The COMPLETE IDIOT'S Guide to

Personal Finance for Canadians ❧

♦ The best reference for the financial novice

♦ Valuable tips to help you earn and save more

♦ Down-to-earth answers to tough money questions

An Alpha Books/Prentice Hall Canada Copublication

Prentice Hall Canada Inc.
Scarborough, Ontario

Bruce McDougall

Canadian Cataloguing in Publication Data

McDougall, Bruce, 1950–
  The complete idiot's guide to personal finance for Canadians

ISBN 0-13-080126-7

1. Finance, Personal – Canada. 2. Financial security. 3. Investments – Canada.
I. Title.

HG179.M325 1998   332.024′01   C97-932751-2

© 1998 Prentice-Hall Canada Inc.
A Division of Simon & Schuster/A Viacom Company

Prentice-Hall, Inc., Upper Saddle River, New Jersey
Prentice-Hall International (UK) Limited, London
Prentice-Hall of Australia, Pty. Limited, Sydney
Prentice-Hall Hispanoamericana, S.A., Mexico City
Prentice-Hall of India Private Limited, New Delhi
Prentice-Hall of Japan, Inc., Tokyo
Simon & Schuster Southeast Asia Private Limited, Singapore
Editora Prentice-Hall do Brasil, Ltda., Rio de Janeiro

ISBN 0-13-080126-7

Director of Trade Publishing: Robert Harris
Production Editor: Mary Ann McCutcheon
Copy Editor: Camille Isaacs
Editorial Assistant: Joan Whitman
Production Coordinator: Julie Preston
Cover Design: Kyle Gell
Cover Image: Masterfile/Damir Frkovic
Page Layout: Gail Ferreira Ng-A-Kien

  2 3 4 5   RRD   02 01 00 99 98

Printed and bound in United States

Visit the Prentice Hall Canada Web site! Send us your comments, browse our catalogues, and more.
www.phcanada.com

To Susan

Contents

Preface

Four years have passed since the first edition of this book was published, and it's still called an Idiot's Guide. That's not just because it's written by an idiot (based on information provided by a really smart guy) but also because it's written in a way that's so easy to understand that any idiot could read it and learn something. But you don't have to be one to use it.

In fact, you'd be an idiot if you didn't use at least some of the information in these pages. I know I have. In the next year, you'll likely earn some money, or put some money in a bank account, or think about contributing to an RRSP, or rent an apartment, or buy some insurance. And from time to time, you'll wonder why you don't have more money to play with.

This book covers all of that and more. By reading even a few passages in a few chapters, you might even end up with more money at the end of the year than you started with. At the very least, you'll find the addresses to some cool web sites where you can find out about what you're missing if you're not trying to invest your money.

Doo-dads, Gimmicks, Thingamabobs, etc.

Throughout this book, you'll find a lot of little shaded boxes with words in them and titles like Learn and Earn and Facts for a Buck. To attract your attention, they're all dressed up in fancy typographical clothing, with symbols:

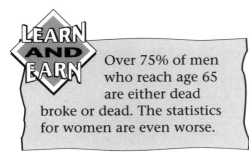

LEARN AND EARN Over 75% of men who reach age 65 are either dead broke or dead. The statistics for women are even worse.

DOLLARS AND SENSE $¢$¢$¢$¢ The average smoker goes through about three packs of cigarettes a week. Each pack costs about $3.50.

High Interest

Tomorrow may take care of itself, but it won't take care of you. Only you can do that by paying yourself first.

Money Talks

It doesn't matter how much money you make. If you earn a little, then spend a little less and invest the difference.

Facts for a Buck

About 8 million Canadians own credit cards. Most own more than one. As a matter of fact, most Canadians own an average of three cards.

These are worth reading. They're worth clipping from the book and framing so you can hang them on your wall. Or you can keep them in your wallet along with your baby pictures to impress your friends.

After you've looked through these pages, you'll want to keep this book close by. Next time your mother asks you why you invested in gold mining stock instead of gold, or why you borrowed money to invest in your RRSP instead of paying down your mortgage, or why you sold your bonds and invested the proceeds in a money market mutual fund, you won't have to think about your answer. Just hand her this book instead.

Introduction

In This Chapter

➤ Why do I need this book?

➤ Are the money strategies easy to understand?

➤ What keeps us from getting what we want?

➤ How can I get started right away?

Why Do I Need This Book?

Even after they've had almost four years to read this book, most Canadians can still think of only four ways to accumulate a lot of money. That's because only 20,000 people bought this book. The rest of you — well, I don't even want to tell you what I think. You still think the only ways to make money are to marry it, win it, steal it, or work day and night for the next 30 years, wearing the same cheap shirt and wrinkled pair of slacks without spending a penny on yourself.

As an alternative, you can be like most Canadians and resign yourself to a life of floundering in a pool of debt, hoping that your weekly paycheque will be enough to keep your head above water. Once in a while, you'll think your ship might come in, but in most cases it'll just be a little tugboat towing a huge bargeload of debt behind it.

OK, enough with the metaphors already.

So the days and weeks fly forward like the lyrics to a bad rock 'n' roll song, and our bank accounts struggle to catch up. We hear about financial planning, but we never take the time to find out what it's all about because we're too busy dealing with the consequences of having no plan at all. (Read it over again, Roger, if you don't get it.) Or, if we take the time to learn more about planning, we never act on it, because it sounds too complicated.

Well, here's a surprise. Managing your money can be easy. It can even be fun. (Gag me with a spoon, Granny.) And like the traveler on the longest journey, all you have to do to get started is take the first step. Wah-hoo!

LEARN AND EARN

You are not rich when you make a lot of money; you are rich when you make your money work for you. That's what this book is about: making your money work for you, so that some day you won't have to work for your money.

The money strategies that you're about to learn are nothing more than common sense. Common sense, common knowledge, and workable money strategies: that's what you'll find inside this book. Inside yourself, you'll have to find something else: the perseverance to follow through. That's the hard part.

The easy part is learning how to invest your money. The fun part is watching your money grow (and reading this book, or writing it, as the case may be). That's where this book becomes so important. (Nominate Michael Reardon for a Nobel Prize. He has a nicer personality than Lloyd Axworthy.)

If you're serious about mastering once and for all the fundamental strategies that it takes to win the money game, then keep on reading. In fact, you can even read this book, then invest some money, then come back and read this book again while your money's growing and you're in the bathtub soaking your dogs.

Maybe this isn't the first book you've read about personal finance. But you probably found the others too boring and about as easy to understand as an exam in nuclear physics. That's why half the people who open a personal finance book never finish it. (And why almost none of them are nuclear physicists.) And fewer than 10% ever follow up on the advice they read. (Reardon has the source for this data. Don't ask me.)

They're not all slow readers or independently wealthy or dead. It's just that most financial books are written for people who already have a basic understanding of investment principles. Unfortunately, most people who read these books don't. (Neither do the guys who write them, but I'll never tell.)

That's what makes this book different. This book is about the basics of financial planning. If you ever thought you weren't smart enough to manage your money effectively, think again. You are. You just have to learn the basics. And that's what this book will teach you. (If you still need convincing, just take a look at the gormless idiot who's writing this book. He doesn't know from stocks. But he manages to keep a roof over his head, some money in the bank and the wolves from the door. And believe me, the wolves in downtown Toronto get fierce in winter. You bet. Fierce like a grizzly bear. Wo-boy.)

Attitude, Not Aptitude

You have to get in the right state of mind before you can accumulate wealth. That means unloading all the mental baggage that stands between you and financial success. Stop thinking:

➤ "My granddaddy was poor, and my pappy was poor, and by golly my kids are going to be poor too!"

Or:

➤ "If I start investing, it will take up too much of my time."

Or:

➤ "I'd like to start an investment program so that someday I'll be able to buy the things I really want, or travel around the world, or start my own business. But why do I have to work so hard to get the extra money I need to begin?"

With attitudes like these, people sabotage themselves before they even get started. Their brain doesn't know whether to move forward or back. They get stuck in a rut, and they don't do anything at all.

That's what I call *No Chance* financial planning. If you keep on doing what you've always been doing, you're going to keep on getting what you've always been getting.

As a first step in changing your attitude about accumulating

After studying 3.5 million American millionaires, researcher Thomas Stanley concluded that the key to being rich is to hold onto one's money. In financial terms, that's called capital preservation. The typical rich person owns a small business, cultivates financial security and independence, and doesn't show many outward signs of wealth.

wealth, you should think about money. Do you call it "cold hard cash"? Well, it isn't cold and it isn't hard. It's soft and warm, and it feels great! It's beautifully coloured. It complements anything you wear, and the more you have, the more compliments you'll get.

Do you think money's the root of all evil? You're dead wrong. The root of all evil is no money. Look around the world, and you'll find war and poverty and sickness and ignorance in places where there's no money. You'll also find these conditions in wealthy countries. But at least the people in those countries have a fighting chance of overcoming their poverty. In poor countries, they don't.

Of course, money isn't everything. There's also stocks, bonds, gold, and real estate. But money's a great consolation until you have everything else.

Take What You Have and Do the Best You Can with It

The rich get richer, and the rest of us feel lucky to find a quarter on the sidewalk. But why do the rich get richer? Because they don't spend everything they have. They take what they have and invest it in a way that will create more.

Rich people say, "How can I invest this money today in a way that will guarantee my financial abundance tomorrow?" The rest of us say, "Charge it!"

That's the difference. When rich people come into a large sum of money, their first thought is how to double or triple the money. When the rest of us come into a large sum of money, our first thought is how we can spend it.

Before you know it, we have a brand new Ford pick-up truck parked in the driveway next to the new extension on our home. And a few years down the road, we're in worse financial shape than we were before we came into the money in the first place. Was it worth it? Did we have more fun than the guy who saved his money and made it grow? Maybe. But when the money runs out, the fun's over.

Remember, it's not how much you have now that counts. It's what you do with it.

But I Don't Have Enough Money to Start Investing

Most people think that if they can't afford to save 10%, then there's no point in saving anything at all. Nothing could be further from the truth. If you can save 10% of your money, that's fantastic. If you can save 5%, that's amazing. If all you can save is 2%, then keep up the good work. The less money you have to start with, the more there is to get!

You may think you don't have enough to start investing. But in fact, you don't have enough money *not* to start investing, right now. Can you save $1 a day? "Sure," you say, "but what good is that going to do me?" What about $3.25 a day? That's the price of two coffees, a donut, and a newspaper. If that's within your reach, think about this:

➤ $3.25 a day adds up to about $100 a month;

➤ in 10 years, you'll have $21,000;

➤ in 20 years you'll have $75,000; and

➤ in 25 years you'll have $125,000, assuming a 16% annual return on your money.

You Must, You Must, You Must Save Money for Investing

We don't always get what we want, but we always get what we must have. Most of us make a point of eating two or three meals a day,

DOLLARS AND SENSE
$ ¢ $ ¢ $ ¢ $

"From shirtsleeves to shirtsleeves in three generations," goes the saying. The first generation works in their shirtsleeves to make enough money for their sons and daughters to take it easy. The sons and daughters are less frugal, and their sons and daughters, who see their parents clipping coupons for a living, think that money grows on trees. By the third generation, everyone has forgotten how the first generation got rich. All they can do is spend it, because no one taught them how to save. Too bad they didn't read this book!

for example. How come? Because if we don't eat, we'll get hungry, and that's painful. No matter how bad it gets, most of us will find a way to get enough money to eat. It's a must!

When it comes to saving money to invest, you have to make it a must. Unfortunately, many of us put saving money to invest at the bottom of our priority list, somewhere behind making a regular appointment with the dentist and writing a letter to Uncle Edgar to thank him for the socks.

The day you put saving money at the top of your list of "must-do" activities, you'll begin your journey toward financial abundance.

Plan Your Work and Work Your Plan

For most of us, our plan goes something like this: We get up in the morning, schlep into work, schlep home at night, have a little dinner, watch some TV, pay a few bills, then hit the sack because we've had a hard day. But because we're too busy worrying about the bills we should have paid but didn't, we can't fall asleep. That's called no-dose, which stands for no-dough-induced insomnia.

As the explorer said to his partner as the cannibals held them over a pot of boiling water, "What we need is a plan."

How do you develop an effective investment plan? You start by setting some realistic financial goals. That means identifying your goals for the short term, the intermediate term, and the long term. How much wealth do you want to accumulate this year? Over the next five years? Over the next 10 and 20 years? What's your lifetime financial goal?

Most of us haven't spent more than 25 or 30 years on the planet. How can we be expected to look that far into the future when we haven't even been here that long? Well, that's the difference between the Average Joe and the exceptional person who ends up financially comfortable and secure. It really takes nothing more than a little imagination. Imagine yourself in a house where the roof doesn't leak, the plumbing works, and there's food in the fridge. Now imagine yourself in a house where the roof leaks, the toilet's clogged, and the fridge is full of cobwebs. Where would you prefer to live? Good answer. You've just started your long-term plan.

You have to understand clearly why you want to become

financially independent. Once you know the whys, the how tos will take care of themselves.

Don't Plan to Save, Plan to Spend

To invest successfully, you have to start paying attention to where your money goes. Forget about budgeting. For most people, budgets just don't work. What you really need is a spending plan.

You need to figure out, in advance, how much money you will spend in each category of your life, so that you won't get caught up with your money down.

What Does Financial Independence Mean for You?

You've attained financial independence when your money generates enough interest to live at your current lifestyle (or better) for the rest of your life, without ever having to work again unless you want to. For some of us, that means $50,000 a year. For others, it means $25,000 or $100,000. Each of us has to figure out an ideal amount.

Let's assume that $50,000 a year will do the trick. If you can earn an 8% return on your money, you'll need to accumulate about $625,000. That may seem like a lot now. But it's well within the reach of most Canadians, even those of us who have only a small amount to invest. All you need are the simple strategies that you'll find in this book and the power of compounding growth.

Over the course of our economic future, we'll encounter boom times and busts. We'll have explosive growth and soul-numbing recessions. But it's not what happens in the economy that determines your financial future. It's what you do that makes the difference.

Unfortunately, the dollar doesn't come with instructions. But this book does. So keep on reading, because you're about to learn how to make sense out of your dollars.

Investment Philosophy: Who Needs It?

No matter who you are or what you do, you will make good investments and bad investments over the course of your lifetime. Good investments are easy to deal with. It's those dad-blasted bad investments that are tough to handle. Your investment philosophy will determine how you handle those future ups and downs, so you might as well develop it now.

If your philosophy is to give up after your first bad investment, then you're in trouble. You'll never achieve your financial dream. However, if your philosophy is to learn from your mistakes, change your approach, and then get back up to bat so that you can take another cut at the ball, then you'll be unstoppable.

Remember, your investment philosophy will influence your investment decisions, and those decisions will shape your financial destiny.

My Personal Investment Philosophy

You don't win 'em all and you don't lose 'em all. You just keep on fighting. If you make a mistake, admit it and move on. When a loss comes your way, take it, with no feelings. (Investment is to the brain what love is to the heart: It's all or nothing.)

Never Invest in Anything That Keeps You Up at Night

For most people, investing is a very emotional affair. The more risk involved, the more emotional it becomes. Unfortunately, emotion and objectivity are inversely related: The more emotional you become, the less objective you are.

Emotion is to investing what gasoline is to fire — dangerous. To avoid sending your investment strategy up in flames, you have to determine how much risk you can tolerate and invest in vehicles that correspond to your risk threshold. Don't buy shares in Slick Willy's Diamond Mine if you can't bear the thought of losing your entire investment.

How do you know where your threshold lies? Here's a good rule of thumb: If you can't concentrate on your job, sleep at night, or stop worrying about your investments, then you've probably exceeded your risk threshold. If you can't think of opening the stock pages tomorrow without salivating, then you're too emotionally involved.

You have to be selective in choosing your investments. Yet many people jump into the first investment that comes along, without even considering the risk involved. Only after they start losing money do they say, "Gee honey, maybe we shouldn't have listened to your cousin Sheldon when we cashed in our RRSP to buy Moose Pasture Mines?"

No Risk, No Reward

You may not want to lose sleep over your investments or listen to your stomach churning as you sit on the bus reading the stock pages. But if you can't accept a little risk, you'll never accumulate many rewards. If you can't tolerate any more risk than you find in a Canada Sucker (whoops! I mean Canada Savings) Bond, then you've got a problem. Your money will not be working to its full potential. You'll have to settle for doubling your money every 12 to 14 years, when you could be doubling it every 4 to 6 years.

There's nothing wrong with a few low-risk investments. Every portfolio should have some. If your more aggressive investments underperform your expectations, those low-risk investments will still provide you with some economic security.

However, some investments can earn you 20% to 40% or more annually. But they come with a slightly higher risk of losing your money. Later, I'll show you how to cut your risk substantially, while maximizing your gains. For now, all you have to do is determine how much risk you can comfortably tolerate.

But How Do I Know What to Invest In?

I was 17 years old and working in a drug store when I made my first investment. Somehow, an investment boiler shop — where slick-talking salesmen with greasy foreheads try to cram dubious investments down the throats of innocent grandmothers and children like me — got my name. Every few weeks, this investment firm would send its latest newsletter to the store where I worked.

LEARN AND EARN

People who invest on impulse become nervous wrecks, usually poor ones. Financial planning is supposed to free you from the torment of anxiety while gaining you some financial freedom as well. You don't want to risk your emotional wealth today for an uncertain financial future tomorrow.

At the time, it seemed very convincing. Each issue included a description, illustrated with a graph, of some oil well or gold mine that the company had recommended a few years back at 10¢ a share; now it was supposedly worth $10 a share.

After a few months of newsletters, a salesman started calling me at work with his latest recommendations. Being young and naive, I didn't put up much resistance. Fortunately, Willie, the pharmacist, was at the back of the store. He was old, wise, and always reading *The Wall Street Journal* behind the counter. When I told him what I'd done, he let me have it. "Call them right back," he said, "and cancel the trade! Send them a registered letter too, right away!" He scared me half to death. Suddenly I envisioned losing my $2,000 in life savings, and I probably would have, had I not followed Willie's advice.

What's the moral of the story? Before you lay out any of your hard-earned money to buy an investment, check it out first.

Education Is Critical

There are literally hundreds of investment opportunities available. Many of them are lousy, and it's up to you to determine the potential advantages, disadvantages, and risks associated with each.

Do you want to invest in baseball cards? (I don't think so.) How about gold coins? (No thanks.) Stocks and bonds? (Maybe a little later.) Mutual funds? (Now you're cooking with gas.)

Whatever you do, don't buy anything just because some guy in a pinstriped suit says you should. Don't take his word for it. Inform yourself. You alone educate yourself about the different investment opportunities available. You just have to take the time to do it.

If You Don't Understand It, Don't Buy It!

Do you want to know a sure way to lose money? Just go out and invest in something that you don't understand. There are plenty of sharks out there who will eat you up alive. They're just waiting for people like you and me to bet the mortgage on something that we know nothing about. The bottom line is this: Either educate yourself or keep your money in the bank.

Buy Value, Not Hype

One of the basic rules of successful money management is never buy stock, invest only in companies. If your brother-in-law gives you a typical hot tip about a sure thing that can't possibly go down the toilet, he may be right and he may be wrong. You'll never know unless you find out more about the company, from someone other than your brother-in-law.

In the meantime, if you're the last man on the deal team, you can rest assured that the big money has already been made. The price that you pay is probably a lot more than the company's actually worth.

In fact, nine times out of 10, by the time you read about a stock in *The Financial Post* or elsewhere in the news, you'll end up paying retail when you buy it. And when it comes to investments, the retail price is too much. You want to buy below retail. You want to buy wholesale. That way, you can get some real value for your money.

Home, Sweet Home

Why is a house the most profitable investment that some people ever make? It's not because real estate skyrocketed in the eighties, although that helped. What really makes the difference is the game plan that people follow prior to buying a home.

LEARN AND EARN

Forget the hype, and focus on the facts. When your only reason for buying an investment is a quick buck, you'll get caught up in the emotion of the moment, rather than long-term growth over a lifetime.

Before you buy any investment, develop a list of criteria that the investment must meet before you part with any of your money. (We'll discuss some of these criteria in later chapters.)

In addition, make sure that you feel emotionally comfortable with your decision. If all you do is make money from your investment, that's fine. But if you really believe in what you're investing in and can have fun at the same time, then you'll come out a winner no matter what happens.

They take all the right steps. First, they define what they really want. They set goals, and they list the criteria that must be met before they'll take action. They say, "What we need is a three-bedroom, two-bathroom house, with a modern kitchen and large backyard. It must be close to a school in a safe neighbourhood, and we're not paying a dime more than $200,000."

Second, they usually hire real estate experts. They'll pay an inspector to check the property for any structural flaws and defects. They'll hire a lawyer to check the contract to make sure that all the terms of the agreement are in order.

Third, they must feel emotionally comfortable with the house before they buy it. They know that, no matter what happens in the real estate market over the short term, they'll enjoy living in their house. They're not just paying the price, they're enjoying it. The thought of buying today and selling tomorrow is out of the question.

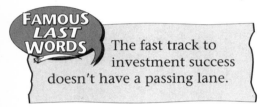

FAMOUS LAST WORDS

The fast track to investment success doesn't have a passing lane.

Fourth, they buy and hold for the long term. The people who lose money in real estate are the ones who see everyone else making money and then decide to jump on the bandwagon to make a quick buck by flipping their property. That's impulsive, not smart, and it's a big mistake.

"But I Want to Make Money Fast!"

Most of us bring the same fast-paced expectations to our investments as our careers: go, go, go, hurry, hurry, hurry. With investments, that's a big mistake. The faster you try to make money from investments, the more likely you are to lose it.

Go, go, go will only lead to your money being gone, gone, gone. In fact, forget altogether about get-rich-quick schemes. There aren't any, and there never have been.

Building wealth is a long-term process, and you must bring to it a long-term attitude. Patience and discipline are the words to live by. It's hard work to give up the fast-buck mentality and think long term. But success comes before work only in the dictionary. If you want to better your investment lot, you'll have to invest a lot better. To do that, start thinking long term.

You'll Never Have To Yearn as Long as You Think Long Term

If you look at the top money managers over the past 20 years — people like John Templeton, Peter Lynch, and Warren Buffet — you'll find that they were rarely number one over the short term. As a matter of fact, many times they actually lagged behind the competition. But over the long term, the Templetons and the Buffets beat the pants off the rest of the crowd.

How can that be? Every single year they followed the same long-term strategy, the same tried-and-true principles. Some years were up, and some years were down, but the profits continued to grow, year by year. At the end of the day, when the tally was taken, these long-term money managers had profits three to four times greater than the market average.

To be really successful, you need a long-term plan.

How come the Japanese have led the pack when it comes to business accomplishments? The answer lies in the way they plan their strategy. While we're focusing on the results of the next quarter, the Japanese are planning strategies a century down the road.

To Shepherd Your Capital, Move Away from the Flock

The most successful money managers take a contrarian approach to investing. That means when a majority of people jump on the bandwagon, they jump off. Or, when the majority jumps off, they jump on.

The basic premise is that the majority is always wrong. That may sound undemocratic, but in financial markets at least, it happens to be true. (In fact, if the majority was always right, we'd have heroes for politicians. But that's another story.)

If you want to be a successful investor, you have to find real value when nobody else wants it; then, when everybody else wants it, sell it to them and take your money. That's how a successful investor named John Templeton did it, investing not only his money but other people's as well. Time and time again he has said that his success has come from buying companies that have real value when they're unpopular and selling them when they become popular. And as we've mentioned, he invests in companies, not stocks.

Never Buy Out of Greed and Sell Out of Fear

After a successful market rally, many investors start suffering from the greed bug. Once you've been bitten by the greed bug, the party's over.

The greedier you become, the more emotional you become. In fact, greed is one of the seven deadly sins because it violates our own self-governance and places us at the mercy of a passion beyond our control. The more emotional you become, the less objective you become. The less objective you become, the faster your money will slip out of your hands into somebody else's.

The best antidote to the greed bug is a good dose of patience and discipline. Patience and discipline may not get the blood pumping and the adrenaline flowing like good old greed, but they allow us to maintain an even pace.

If something is a good investment today, it's probably going to be a good investment tomorrow. It's the people who think they've got to buy it now who usually sell first out of fear and buy last out of greed.

The classic example: the stock market crash of October 1987. Did everybody lose money when the market crashed? Of course not. Did some people actually make money? You bet. Who were the biggest losers? The ones who bought late in the game and paid over-inflated prices. When the crash was over, stocks that were previously selling at retail were now selling at wholesale prices.

Did the people who bought real value prior to the crash lose money when the market tumbled? No. People who maintained their long-term investment philosophy didn't lose money. Sure they had some temporary paper losses. But within a short while, the stock market rebounded, and they recovered all their previous losses.

Money Doesn't Sleep

It's time to wake up and get crackin'. The sooner you can start, the better. In fact, here's a challenge: Within the next 90 days, start your wealth-

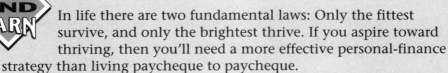

In life there are two fundamental laws: Only the fittest survive, and only the brightest thrive. If you aspire toward thriving, then you'll need a more effective personal-finance strategy than living paycheque to paycheque.

If you want serious investment returns, you'll need serious information. That's what this book is all about: what you should look for and look out for.

building plan. In no time at all, you'll be able to invest with the best.

I want you to become one of the few who do, versus the many who just read.

Read It and Reap

> ➤ You must make saving money to invest a MUST.

> ➤ Wealth is a state of mind. Get rid of your mixed emotions regarding accumulating wealth.

> ➤ Develop and follow through on a consistent plan for accumulating long-term wealth.

> ➤ Write down your short-, intermediate-, and long-term goals.

> ➤ Understand the reasons why you want to accumulate wealth.

> ➤ Develop an effective investment philosophy.

> ➤ Understand why no risk equals no reward.

> ➤ Educate yourself about all the different investments available today.

> ➤ Never invest in anything that you don't understand.

> ➤ Never invest in anything that keeps you awake at night.

> ➤ Invest only in real value, not just what everybody else is buying.

> ➤ Always invest for long-term success.

➤ Buy investments when they're unpopular, and then turn around and sell them when they become popular.

➤ Learn to manage your emotions and avoid the greed bug.

➤ Money doesn't sleep, so get your personal finance program started today.

"and then I'm upgrading my hatchback to an Infiniti and I'm sending my children........ ......Money Talks..."

Chapter 1

Saving: To Save or Not to Save, That Is Accumulation!

In This Chapter

➤ Why should I start?

➤ What's stopping me?

➤ How should I do it?

➤ The rule of 72

The Secret of Investment Success

Investment success boils down to a single strategy: Spend less than you make.

That's it? No, but that's 90% of the secret.

What's the other 10%?

Invest productively.

But that's the easy part. The hard part is having the discipline to follow a savings program.

I can show you people who earn $100,000, even $250,000 a year, who have nothing left to show for it. How can that be? Because no

1

Money Talks

It doesn't matter how much money you make. If you earn a little, then spend a little less and invest the difference.

matter how much you earn, you can always spend more. In economics, this is known as the marginal propensity to save. In real life, it's called dumb.

As soon as most Canadians make enough to live comfortably, they want to live extravagantly. They haven't yet learned that the easiest way to stay poor is to pretend to be rich.

Why Bother? You Can't Take It with You

Forget about when you die. Most Canadians can't save their money while they're still here. Young people put off saving till they're older. Older people put off saving till they're married. Married people put off saving till the kids come along. Parents put off saving till the kids grow up. And by then, the kids have spent it.

LEARN AND EARN

Over 75% of men who reach age 65 are either dead broke or dead. The statistics for women are even worse. Over 80% of women who reach age 65 require financial assistance. How many folks end up financially secure? About three in every 100. Those three people saved themselves. The other 97 have to be saved — from the poorhouse

In another 25 years, the cost of living will probably double. If you're 55 or younger, you'll likely never see an old age security cheque. By the time you retire, the government will have taken it all back.

What's Holding You Back?

Most of us know that we should start saving, but we don't. Why? Because we never make saving a must. We live paycheque to paycheque, with too much month left over at the end of our money.

We're so busy paying everybody else that we put off paying ourselves. But you work hard for your money. You deserve to keep some of it.

Living Within Your Credit

There's plenty of money around. The trouble is that everybody owes it to everybody else.

High Interest

Tomorrow may take care of itself, but it won't take care of you. Only you can do that, by paying yourself first.

The real problem isn't how to live within your income; it's how to live within your credit. Credit is simply a clever financial trick that enables us to spend what we haven't got.

Canadians can be divided into three classes: the haves, the have nots, and the have not paid for what they haves. How come? Credit cards.

What is a credit card? A credit card is something you use to buy yesterday what you can't afford today while you're still paying for it tomorrow. You must learn how to manage your credit cards, or else your credit cards will end up managing you.

Do you know what the average credit card charges on overdue payments? Today, it's about 20%. How much can most people afford to pay? — 9% to 10% tops.

Most Canadians will blow their brains out trying to pay down their credit cards with 20% interest charges. At 20%, it takes only 3.6 years for the outstanding amount on a credit card to double.

Money Talks

If all you do is make the minimum monthly payments, it will take about eight years to pay off a $1,000 balance.

Facts for a Buck

About 8 million Canadians own credit cards. Most own more than one. As a matter of fact, most Canadians own an average of three cards.

Use It, But Don't Abuse It

Let's face it, credit cards are great, providing you use them to your advantage. Where else can you get a one-month interest-free loan?

Strategy 1

If you're one of the 50% of Canadians who regularly pay off their monthly balances on time, then you should get rid of your credit cards that charge an annual fee and switch to credit cards that charge no annual or user fees.

Now if you're not paying off your monthly balance on time, then the credit card companies are stinging you with 18% to 24% interest charges. Those interest charges are the bread and butter of the credit card companies. No wonder they've been very reluctant to lower them.

However, over the past few years, some banks have come out with low-interest credit cards. These include Royal Bank, Bank of Montreal, and Bank of Nova Scotia. They charge an annual fee of $25 to $29. But if you're one of those 50% who *doesn't* pay off their monthly balance on time, you have to seriously consider getting one.

Strategy 2

If you don't pay off your credit card in full every month, you should transfer your debts from your regular card to a new low-interest card. That way, you'll be paying off the old credit card with the new one. Instead of paying 18% to 20% interest charges, you'll be paying only $10\frac{1}{2}$% to $11\frac{1}{2}$%. That's called financial planning!

Budget Schmudget!

The only budget in Canada that's making money is Budget-Rent-A-Car. That's because budgets don't usually work. All a budget does is tell us what we can't afford. It doesn't keep us from buying it.

If you really want to develop that millionaire mentality, stop thinking in terms of budgeting and start thinking in terms of spending. That's right, spending. Instead of a budget, develop a spending plan. You'll still buy what you were buying before, but you'll spend less. And the less money you spend, the more you'll have to invest.

Facts for a Buck

Most of us shop at the supermarket on Friday or Saturday. But guess which day the toilet paper runs out. Thursday. Guess which day the kitchen light bulb burns out. Thursday. Guess when we run out of cat food. Thursday. Guess when most of us spend 30% more than we need to on groceries. You got it: Thursday. That's the day when most of us make our weekly trip to the convenience store. Wait one more day, and we'll each have 30% more in our pockets when we carry our groceries out the door.

The Plan, Stan

To get rich, you need to plan ahead. You can start by setting aside Wednesday's and Saturday's supermarket ads. Find out who has the best deals. Are there any coupons that could save you money on products you already use?

Many people throw out coupons like junk mail. The manufacturers know this. They know that half the people will use the coupons, and the other half will pay full retail. Those folks who pay full retail are subsidizing those of us who use coupons. Do you want to go on subsidizing everybody else? Then keep on throwing out those coupons.

If you want to win at the money game, then stock up on things when they go on sale. I'm not talking about nachos and potato chips. I'm talking about non-perishables like soap, detergent, and toilet paper. The trick is to buy now, so you can save later.

DOLLARS AND SENSE $¢$¢$¢$¢

The small savings today add up to big results down the road.

- Instead of buying your newspaper at the corner store for 50 cents, get a subscription to your office or home. The difference could save you about $30 a year.

- If you have a fridge at work, buy the 1-L container of milk for only $1.69, instead of the smaller 250-mL container for 85 cents. The difference could save you about $250 a year.

- Do you buy your lunch every day? You probably spend about $25 to $30 a week. Try making some of your meals at home, in advance.

Facts for a Buck

An extra $25 saved each month and invested at 15% annually inside an RRSP will turn into almost $75,000 in 25 years.

Save Now, Spend Later

A good general rule is to try to save 10% of your annual income. Unfortunately, 10% is just too much to save for many Canadians. That's fine. The most important thing is that you do something. Instead of 10%, try saving 5%. If not 5%, how about 3%?

The amount isn't what's important. The timing is. So start now.

If you earn $35,000 a year, let's see how your savings can grow.

INCOME	% SAVED	ANNUAL	MONTHLY	WEEKLY
$35,000	10%	$3,500	$292	$67
$35,000	5%	$1,750	$146	$34
$35,000	3%	$1,050	$88	$20

DOLLARS AND SENSE
$¢$¢$¢$¢   The average smoker goes through about three packs a week. Each pack costs about $3.50. That's about $1o a week or about $500 a year on cigarettes. If you're 30 years old, and you invest that $500 each year in an RRSP earning 15% annually, you'll have more than $250,000 saved up when you turn 65. You'll also have a better chance of reaching 65 in the first place.

6

High Interest

The sooner you start saving, the better. Get this:

- You are 18 years old.
- You have $1,000.
- You invest it in an RRSP that earns 20% a year, compounded annually.
- You plan to retire at age 65.
- You don't touch your $1,000 investment or the interest it earns.

    At age 65, you'll have $5,266,463.20.

More High Interest

If you can save $1 a day in an RRSP from the age of 18, and it earns 15% a year, you'll have about $2 million when you reach the age of 65.

The Rule of 72

Seventy-two is a magical number. Divide 72 by your annual investment return. You'll end up with the number of years it will take to double your money.

Say you earn 6% on your Canada Savings Bond. Divide 72 by 6. You get 12. It will take 12 years to double your money.

If you earn 20% on your money, you'll double it every 3.6 years (72 divided by 20 equals 3.6).

First We Take Manhattan

Most people think the Indians were ripped off back in 1606, when Peter Minuit, the first Director-General of the Dutch Province of New Netherland, bought Manhattan Island from the Man-a-hat-a Indians

The Big Quiz

Here are two investors, Mutt and Jeff.

Mutt waits till he's 26 to start investing. Then he puts $2,000 a year into an RRSP at 15% a year for the next 40 years, come rain or shine, sickness or health, war, famine, pestilence, scurvy, psychosis, obesity, blah, blah, blah.

Jeff read this book when he was 18, so he starts earlier. For seven years, between the ages of 19 and 25, he stashes $2,000 a year in an RRSP. Then he gets married and forgets about the RRSP.

Who has more money when he retires?

Answer: Jeff.

After 40 years of saving, Mutt has just over $4 million and a compulsive ulcer. Not bad. But with only 7 years of saving — at the right time — Jeff has $6.5 million. Yo, Jeff.

for 60 guilders, about $22 in U.S. funds. But if the Indians had invested that money in common stocks on the New Manhattan Stock Exchange, and it earned just 9% a year, they would have more than $300 trillion today.

That's more than the Gross National Product of all the countries in the world put together.

The Inflation Factor

Many people complain that there's no point in saving money because of the ravages of inflation. They figure that, 20 years from now, a Looney will be worth about a penny. Fortunately, it's not going to be quite that bad.

Over the past century, inflation has averaged around 3% to 4% a year. If you want to maintain your current lifestyle 20 years down the road, you'll have to make a few calculations and then plan your investments accordingly. For instance, if you're earning $40,000 a year now, how much will you need to be earning 20 years from now to maintain your current standard of living?

First you need to know the inflation factor. In our example, it's 2.2. (If you want to know how to calculate the inflation factor for different rates, you've got a lot of time on your hands. Go to the library. Go to the Bank of Canada. Go to the hospital and have brain surgery.) Multiply your current yearly salary by the inflation factor to find the equivalent income in 20 years.

$40,000   x   2.2   = $88,000

current yearly   inflation   tomorrow's

salary   factor   need

In 20 years, with inflation averaging 4% a year, you'll have to earn $88,000 to give you earning power comparable to the $40,000 you're earning today.

Family Fortunes

Who manages the money in your family? Your husband? Your wife? Is it a family affair? Or do you just play it by ear?

Usually one spouse takes charge of the money. And when that person unexpectedly leaves or dies, the other has to figure out where the money is, what investments they own, and how much insurance they have. Trust me, it's not a place where you want to end up.

Everyone should be involved in the family fortune, even the kids. That way, in the event of a death or breakup, it will be much easier for the others to pick up the pieces.

Money Talks

Want to know one of the biggest causes of marriage breakup? Not getting clear on who's going to pay for what. "What's yours is mine, and what's mine is mine" is a prescription for disaster. You must decide in advance how you'll divide the money. There are three choices. Let's take a look at each:

1. Ideally, the larger salary pays for the basic expenses — things like the rent or mortgage, hydro, food, insurance, etc. The smaller salary pays for investments, holidays, and unexpected purchases. However, in the real world, it usually takes both salaries just to cover the basics, let alone investments. Still you should try to set aside some money for investment purposes, even if it comes from returning empty bottles.

2. The second scenario involves opening a joint daily-interest savings account. Both spouses deposit all their money into this account. All the bills are paid out of this account. What's left over is used for investments, holidays, and unexpected purchases. In addition, both spouses receive a monthly allowance to spend as they please. But if one spouse contributes significantly more than the other to the joint account, arguments can develop.

3. The third scenario involves running the family finances like a business. Both spouses decide how much money they need each month to cover their day-to-day expenses plus investments and special purchases. Then each spouse contributes a certain percentage of his or her salary to cover those expenses. Each spouse can do what he or she pleases with the remainder of their money. The benefit of this plan is that you don't have to ask anyone's permission to spend the remainder of your money.

Read It and Reap

In this chapter, you learned how a penny saved today can become a Looney tomorrow, give or take a few dozen years. How? Look:

➤ The number one secret of investment success is to spend less than you earn and invest the difference.

➤ It's not how much but whether you save.

➤ Only three out of every 100 people end up financially secure.

➤ Learn to manage your credit cards, or else your credit cards will end up managing you.

➤ Instead of budgeting, develop a spending plan.

➤ If you can't save 10% of your income, than save 5%. If that's too much then save 3%. Even a small amount of money saved regularly can literally turn into a fortune down the road.

➤ The rule of 72 says, "Divide 72 by your annual investment return. The result will be the number of years it takes for your tax-protected money to double."

➤ If inflation averages 4% a year, then in 20 years, the purchasing power of your money will be cut by more than half. So plan ahead.

➤ Make sure that the entire family is involved in the financial planning process.

Chapter 2

Life Insurance: The Term-inator

> **In This Chapter**
> ➤ What is the purpose of life insurance?
> ➤ Should I buy it?
> ➤ How much do I need?
> ➤ What's the difference between term, universal, and whole life?

What Is the Purpose of Life Insurance?

Life insurance protects your financial dependents in the event of your death.

Who Needs Life Insurance?

Anyone who has financial dependents should make sure he or she has sufficient life insurance.

Do Single People with No Financial Dependents Require Life Insurance?

No. I can't imagine why any single person with no financial dependents would even consider life insurance. Yet what do I know? Almost 30% of all insurance is sold to single folks with no financial dependents. Who gets the money if they die? The goldfish?

If you're single, with no dependents, you should invest your money by following the strategies in this book, so you can eventually become self-insured.

Should I Buy Life Insurance on My Kids?

No. Remember, the purpose of life insurance is to protect the family against the loss of the breadwinner's earnings. If your kids don't bring home the bacon, so to speak, then you don't need to insure their lives.

Facts for a Buck

Here's a popular sales pitch for life insurance: If you buy insurance on little kids, then they'll be guaranteed future insurability. The salesman won't tell you that most kids have a 98% chance of being eligible for life insurance when they turn 18, whether or not you buy today.

Do I Need to Insure My Spouse?

If you have no children and both spouses work, you probably don't need life insurance. If you have children, then you should consider low-cost term insurance until the children can support themselves. If your spouse is not earning any income or works only part-time, but is responsible for caring for the children, then life insurance is necessary to cover unexpected child-care expenses.

DOLLARS AND SENSE
$¢$¢$¢$¢   If your children have grown up and left home, your mortgage is all paid off, and most of your debts paid down, then you probably need little, if any, life insurance. If you're retired and your grown-up children still live at home, you should consider kicking them out.

How Much Life Insurance Do I Need?

To determine your life insurance needs, do some simple calculations:

1. Determine how much family income you need each year to maintain your current lifestyle.

2. Figure out how much each spouse contributes to the family income, in money or services.

3. Multiply each spouse's contribution by 10. The 10 represents a 10% minimum annual return from your investments.

For instance, if your family requires $50,000 a year to maintain their current lifestyle, then do this: $50,000 x 10 = $500,000.

Your family needs $500,000 worth of life insurance. If the money were invested at 10%, the family could maintain their current lifestyle.

What Are My Life Insurance Alternatives?

There are three main alternatives: term, whole life, and universal life insurance.

Over 80% of Canadians have either whole life or universal life insurance policies. Most Canadians don't know it, but whole life policies are from the Stone Age. They're the kind of thing that Joe Rockhead would sell. Do you know why they call them whole life policies? Because all your money ends up in a hole.

About 70 years ago, there was only one type of life insurance available. It was called death insurance. You paid your premiums, named your beneficiary, died, and then the kids fought over the assets.

But there was a problem. The insurance companies wanted to make more money. The answer was investments.

They decided to combine the sale of insurance with an investment plan. That way, they could raise their prices about 1,000% and put up some nice tall insurance buildings around town.

If you've ever bought a whole life policy and you have a chance to go into one of those buildings, take a marker and write your name on a marble wall in the lobby. You deserve it, because you own a piece of that building.

What Is Whole Life Insurance?

It is simply life insurance with a savings plan attached to it. The savings are called the cash value of the plan.

For example: If you take your typical $100,000 whole-life policy for a 35-year-old, it will probably cost you about $1,300 each year. In the first year, the agent's commission is about 900 bucks. The average annual interest paid to your savings plan or cash value is about 2% to 4%.

After paying a $1,300 yearly premium for 20 years, you'll have paid $26,000 in premiums. If you earn 3% annually, your plan will have a cash value of about $35,000. That's not much to show for 20 years of saving.

What Can You Do with the Cash Value?

Since it's your own money in there, the insurance company will let you borrow it, and charge you only about 5% in interest. What a deal! You get to pay interest to borrow your own money. The amount that you don't pay back will be subtracted from the death benefit that your beneficiaries receive.

What About the Dividends That the Insurance Company Pays?

If you receive dividend payments from your life insurance policy, you have a participating policy. If you don't receive any dividend payments, you have a non-participating policy.

In most cases, the dividends that you receive are not returned profits but rather your own money that you overpaid in premiums in the first place. To top it all off, Revenue Canada doesn't even acknowledge these dividends, so you'll pay taxes on them just as you would pay taxes on interest income.

What Is Universal Life Insurance?

This is a life insurance policy with a lousy investment vehicle attached to it. The investment vehicle usually pays a fixed rate of interest. Sometimes it takes the form of a stock mutual fund.

Many policies promise to pay you 8% to 10% on your investment. Nice try. You may get 8% to 10%, but it will be calculated on what's left of your money after everything else is deducted.

The typical $100,000 universal life insurance policy will cost you about $2,000 a year in premiums. You may think, "Wow, if I earn 10% a year on my investment, I'll earn $200 in the first year ($2,000 x 10%)." Don't hold your breath.

During the first year, about $600 will go just to cover fees and commissions. So right from the start, you can kiss about 30% of your initial $2,000 goodbye.

Another $300 will pay for the actual life insurance coverage. How much of your $2,000 is left? About $1,100. That's how much of your money will actually earn the promised 8% to 10% return in the first year.

As a matter of fact, throughout the first 10 years, your premiums will probably earn under 6% annually. That's because, as the years go by, the cost of your insurance keeps going up and up. Most people never realize this, because their premiums don't change. But of the premium you pay each year, less and less will actually go toward your investment plan.

To top it all off, those old boys who sell the universal policies will sting you with a big surrender charge if you decide to cancel. Don't forget the rule of thumb: the smaller the front-end load fees, the bigger the surrender charges.

Strategy

Intelligent investors never buy universal life policies. Your strategy should be to buy term life insurance and invest the difference yourself.

What Is Term Life Insurance?

Term life insurance has no savings or investment vehicle attached to it. It is the lowest-priced life insurance available. It is a temporary form of insurance that provides coverage when you need it, and the option to cancel when you no longer need it.

Term insurance is a lot like car or house insurance: You don't collect unless something happens. In this case, you have to die.

Typically, $100,000 of term life insurance coverage for 10 years will cost about $150 in yearly premiums. The yearly premium for a $100,000 whole life policy is about $1,300. Now you can see why I recommend term insurance.

What Are the Different Types of Term Insurance?

There are three types of term policies that you should be familiar with: yearly renewable term, decreasing term, and level premium term.

➤ **Yearly Renewable Term** This is just what it says: a life insurance policy for just one year, at the end of which you either renew for another year or cancel. Although the premiums will increase each year as you age, this plan remains the cheapest type of term insurance.

Your renewal is guaranteed each year to age 90, providing you pay your premiums on time.

If you have only a short-term need for life insurance, then yearly renewable term is your best bet.

➤ **Decreasing Term Insurance** Your yearly premiums stay the same, but the amount of life insurance coverage decreases each year. Eventually your yearly premiums become very overpriced. This type of term insurance is not a good deal.

➤ **Level Premium Term Insurance** If you have long-term life insurance needs, this is your best choice. You select the length of coverage you want — 10-, 15-, or 20-year term, even 100 years. Your yearly premiums and the amount of life insurance coverage remain the same for the length of the term.

What About Mortgage Life Insurance?

Mortgage life insurance will pay off the outstanding amount of your mortgage if you die. Who wouldn't want that? You wouldn't want your family to have to sleep in the street if you kicked off, would you?

How much does it cost? About $30 to $50 a month per $100,000 of mortgage principal.

Sounds like a reasonable price to pay. But let's look more closely at the figures. If you die 20 years from now, you'll have perhaps $15,000 left to pay on today's $100,000 mortgage. Your death triggers the payment of $15,000 to your survivors. That means you've paid $30 to $50 a month for 20 years, so your family can get a measly $15,000 back when you go to the big hacienda in the sky.

It gets even worse if you die in the last year of your mortgage, when you've paid it down to $1,000. After all those years of sweat and toil, with an extra $30 to $50 a month thrown in for protection, your family gets $1,000 back. Thanks, Pop.

Strategy

Here's a better strategy. Buy a $100,000 term life insurance policy, for about $15 a month. If you die in the 20th year of the policy, your family gets $100,000, no matter how much remains of your mortgage. If you've paid off everything but the last $15,000, your family can pay it off with the insurance money and fight over the remaining $85,000. They'll love you for it.

What About Credit Life Insurance?

Whenever we finance a major purchase, the salesperson usually asks us if we want credit life insurance. Here's how it works: You go to your local bank to finance a new car. After you sign a few thousand papers, the banker hands you one more and says, "Of course, you want credit life insurance." You say, "What's that?" The banker says, "If you die, the car payments will be taken care of." You say," Gosh, that's great. Sign me up, chief."

The banker will shake your hand and tell you that you're a responsible person. But if you handled the rest of your finances in such a butt-headed manner, the banker wouldn't let you in the door. Sure, you pay only $8 a month for your credit life insurance. But that's about 700% too much. That's like paying $4 for your 50¢ newspaper.

Instead of credit life insurance, you should buy yearly renewable term life insurance. Your premiums will be about 75% less. If you die, your family will be able to pay for the car and maybe put a few litres of gas in it as well.

What About Extended Warranties?

You go to your local store to buy a camera, a VCR, a TV, or a CD player. As you scratch your head and twiddle the knobs, the salesperson points out the high-quality workmanship, the strength, the durability, the idiot-proof construction, the diodes, the electrodes, the anodes, and the yaddy-yaddy-yaddy. So you pick one, and what do you know? The same salesperson says, "Just in case some idiot breaks this thing, you should get an extended warranty."

> ## High Interest
>
> Your credit card may already include an extended warranty feature if you use it to purchase an item. American Express does. So do many gold cards.

Are extended warranties a good deal? No. For every dollar you pay for one, the manufacturer pays about 15¢. They are overpriced by about 700%.

Disability Blues

If you wake up tomorrow after a sleepless night, put on two different socks and the rest of your clothes that are lying on the floor, grab an apple and your briefcase, rush out the door, and absent-mindedly shuffle into the path of a cement truck, you'll be glad that you have long-term disability insurance.

With disability insurance, you can rely on receiving a portion of

your income if, for some reason (like an encounter with a cement truck) you can't work for a long period of months or years.

A large group of people, like all 35,000 employees of a bank, can buy disability insurance more cheaply than a solitary, lonely, insecure, single, white, bisexual, non-smoking male who likes Beethoven, red wine, and long walks in the park (like that guy looking over your shoulder while you're reading this book). Insurance companies employ hundreds of squinty-eyed actuaries with green visors on their heads and sharp pencils in their hands to calculate the risk involved in insuring large groups against disabling accidents.

Individuals, on the other hand, have no one else to share the risk. So the cost of their disability insurance is higher. But that's no reason not to buy it.

The squinty-eyed guys with the green visors will determine an appropriate price for your policy, depending on your age, health, occupation, and your ability to sing Da-Doo-Ron-Ron in the bathtub. The company will send a nurse to your home to test your blood pressure and listen to you sing.

You should buy enough disability insurance to cover your basic monthly living expenses, or more.

No matter how much it costs, and no matter how much you resent paying hundreds of dollars a year for something that you hope you never have to use, disability insurance is worth having.

Read It and Reap

Life insurance and other types of coverage, as we learned in this chapter, reduce or eliminate the risk that we'll leave behind big debts if we die.

➤ Life insurance should be purchased to protect your financial dependents in the event of your death.

➤ If you're single, with no financial dependents, you don't need life insurance.

➤ As a rule, you should not buy life insurance coverage for little kids.

➤ Two-income families with no dependents need very little life insurance.

➤ If you have children, you should purchase low-cost term insurance until the kids can support themselves.

➤ Make sure you buy enough life insurance so that the benefit, invested at 10% annually, would replace your current contribution to the family income.

➤ Whole life insurance simply has a savings plan attached, called the cash value. Don't bother.

➤ Universal life insurance is term insurance attached to an investment plan. It's not a great deal.

➤ Term life insurance has no savings or investment plans attached. It's usually your best choice.

➤ Choose the right term insurance: yearly renewable or level premium.

➤ Instead of buying mortgage or credit life insurance, buy low-cost term life insurance.

➤ Extended warranties are over-priced.

➤ Disability insurance: If you work from home or run your own business — or if your employer doesn't provide it — buy it.

Chapter 3

Cash Investments: Cautious, Conservative, Canadian, Chicken

In This Chapter

➤ How to use banks to your advantage

➤ The one savings account everyone should own

➤ Is your bank safe?

➤ What's a term deposit? A GIC? A Canada Savings Bond? A mortgage-backed security?

Question: How much money do you have in the bank?
Answer: I don't know, I haven't shaken it lately. (Drums. Cymbals. Kazoo. Raucous laughter. Sound of knee-slapping, snorting, guffawing, etc.)

If all your money is sitting in a piggy-bank upstairs in your room, then you've got a problem. You've got the same problem if all your money is sitting inside a bank savings account. The problem is typically Canadian: Your money might be safe, but it's not doing any work for you.

Canadians are notorious for being "C" investors. We love CDs (certificates of deposit). We love CSBs (Canada Savings Bonds). And we love GICs (guaranteed investment certificates).

For most of us, Cautious and Conservative sums up our entire investment philosophy. And that's fine. But many of us don't know how to use even these fundamental saving guidelines to our best advantage.

The Canadian Way

Although Canadians have discovered the higher returns available from mutual funds, most of us still pack our money away in more conservative places. By 1997, Canadians had invested $273 billion in mutual funds. But we still had $600 billion stashed in GICs, term deposits, chequing accounts, and other guaranteed investments.

Where Do Most Canadians Invest Their Money?

Most Canadians keep their money in bank savings accounts. This is a big financial mistake. The bank may love you, but you're just cheating yourself.

Savings accounts will never pay you enough money in interest to stay ahead of inflation. So you should use them only as a temporary storage place, while you decide what to do with your money.

Facts for a Buck

There's more than one bank savings account open for every person in Canada. A few of us don't have one at all. A lot of us have two or more.

Money Talks

At an interest rate of ¹/₂ of one percent a year — the rate paid on some savings accounts — you'll double your money every 144 years.

DOLLARS AND SENSE
$¢$¢$¢$¢

Banks used to allow us to save our money only in regular savings accounts. If you left your money in the account for long periods, then it worked out fine for you, because the bank paid interest on that amount.

But many investors used their accounts frequently, taking money out and then putting it back. As a result, they seldom collected interest on their money, although the bank could still lend it and charge the borrower daily interest. So the bank got a much better deal than the investor.

Fortunately, banks began offering investors a choice. They could choose either a conventional savings account or a daily interest savings account.

What Kind of Savings Account Do You Have?

Do you have a conventional savings account or a daily interest account? Many of us aren't even sure.

➤ Conventional: Interest is tabulated monthly. Money deposited in a conventional savings account after the first day of the month doesn't earn interest for the entire month.

➤ Daily interest: Money in the account earns interest on the first day that we deposit it and every day after that, until you remove it. Even if we leave it there for only one day, it will still earn interest, at a slightly lower rate than it would earn in a conventional savings account.

Which Savings Account Is Best Suited for My Day-To-Day Needs?

Most of us get paid every two weeks. And we usually deposit our paycheque in the bank after the first day of the month. Then, we're so busy paying bills that our money comes out of the account just about as fast as it goes in. So it makes a lot more sense to calculate interest on a daily basis than to do it once a month, even if the monthly interest is calculated at a rate half a percent higher.

Does It Really Make a Difference?

It may not seem like a lot, but it could cover the cost of a couple of CDs or an extra Christmas present. Say you get paid every two weeks, and your take-home pay is around $900. If your cheque is deposited into a daily interest account earning $2\frac{1}{2}\%$ annually, and if you can leave your cheque in the account for only eight days, you'll earn about 70¢, 26 times each year. That comes to an extra $18 to $20 each year. You get this money for doing nothing more than opening a daily interest savings account rather than a conventional savings account. That's a no-brainer.

Looney Lingo

The YIELD represents the return on your investment. If you earn 5% interest on a Canada Savings Bond, you can say the yield on the bond is 5%.

Strategy 1

Have your paycheque deposited directly into a daily interest savings account. Then withdraw the money as you need it to pay your bills and buy investments.

Strategy 2

Check which bank, trust company, or credit union offers the highest yield on its daily interest savings account and then, providing it's convenient for you, have your money deposited there.

Is Your Money Safe in the Bank?

Keeping your money in Canadian banks, trust companies, or credit unions is very safe. Any institution that displays the Canadian Deposit Insurance Corporation (CDIC) sticker provides guaranteed protection of all funds deposited up to $60,000. If you don't see any sticker displayed, make sure to request proof of CDIC coverage.

How Does CDIC Insurance Work?

Any money that you have in a savings account, chequing account, guaranteed investment certificate (GIC), or term deposit is guaranteed up to $60,000 per institution, not per branch. If you have over $60,000 sitting in a bank, you can get around the guaranteed limit by keeping up to $60,000 in your name, up to $60,000 in your wife's name, up to $60,000 in a joint account and up to $60,000 in an RRSP, all within the same institution and all guaranteed.

What About Credit Unions?

CDIC coverage does not extend to credit unions. However, Provincial Deposit Insurance programs can provide them with insurance coverage of customer accounts up to $60,000 apiece. Ask about this coverage. Many credit unions also allow clients to keep as many RRSPs as they want, guaranteeing the funds in each of them up to $60,000.

Slush for a Rainy Day

In every investment portfolio, between 10% and 50% of the holdings should consist of cash-type investments. I call this the slush fund.

The slush fund provides a safe haven when the market winds start blowing in the wrong direction. It gives you flexibility, liquidity, and peace of mind. If the value of your other investments falls drastically, you can still resort to your slush fund for ready cash to take advantage of other opportunities.

As I'll discuss later, our strategy is to buy low and sell high. So we'll always need some cash to take advantage of lower prices in other areas where we invest. Say the price of pork bellies falls to a ridiculously low level (which shouldn't come as a surprise for something with such a ridiculous name). If we have to sell six pounds of gold to pay for the pork bellies, the price might rise again before we can complete the deal. If we have some cash, we can act on the spur of the moment.

The Going Rate for Slush

Even though we may not get rich from our cash holdings, we can still achieve a respectable rate of return. That's because more people want to use it, even for short periods. And they compete among themselves by offering us better rates.

In general, though, cash doesn't provide a big return, no matter where we keep it. That's because we can claim it at a moment's notice. No one will pay us much for the use of our cash today, if we can take it back again with no explanation tomorrow.

But that's no problem. With a slush fund, we're less concerned about the return *on* our money than we are with the return *of* our money.

What Are My Options?

In general, you can keep your cash relatively handy in deposit accounts, term deposits, guaranteed investment certificates, Canada Savings Bonds, and mortgage-backed securities. (Later, when we talk about mutual funds, we'll discuss some other options, namely Treasury bills, Canadian money market funds, and international money funds.)

▲ A Lesson: The Deposit Account

Under severe competition for your money, financial institutions have come up with high-interest savings accounts. It may be called a premium account, investor account, or cash performance account. Whatever the bank or trust company calls it, the bottom line remains the same: They all provide investors with a higher interest rate on their money than a conventional savings account.

Unfortunately, many institutions require a hefty deposit of at least $25,000 to get a piece of the action. Also, these deposit accounts come with bells and whistles. That means very little, if any, cheque writing; restrictions on withdrawals; and a variable, not fixed, interest rate. In other words, the account may pay 8% when you deposit your money, but there's no guarantee that the interest rate won't drop.

▲ Another Lesson: Term Deposits

A term deposit involves a contract between you and the financial institution. It's usually a short-term contract, for 30 days to one year, although term deposits can extend over five years. Under the contract, you lend your money to the financial institution for a specified period. In return, the financial institution pays you a fixed rate of interest until the contract expires. In general, the longer the term, the higher the interest rate.

Sometimes the interest rate on a term deposit is less than the rate on a premium savings account offered by banks. Also, you can cancel a term deposit prior to maturity, but only if you pay a penalty charge.

There is often a substantial spread between the highest and the lowest rates offered for the same term. So shop around for the best rate of return.

Looney Lingo

Maturity in life arrives when we know the difference between puppy love and true romance. In finance, maturity comes when a contract expires. This moment is called the MATURITY DATE — sort of like a bar mitzvah for investments. But only sort of.

▲ Still Another Lesson: GICs

Guaranteed investment certificates — called GICs (not to be confused with GI Joes) — are similar to term deposits. But GICs usually have longer terms, maturing in one year or more. Most GICs lock up your money (figuratively speaking, of course) for the duration of the contract. Some financial institutions, however, will allow you to cash in a GIC early, if you pay a penalty. So make sure you understand the terms of the contract.

One-, Three-, or Five-year GICs. Oh My, I Just Can't Decide

Invest in them all, at the right time. Here's a strategy to protect you against interest-rate swings. Instead of putting all your money into just one five-year GIC at today's low rates, you should buy five GICs of equal value, but stagger the maturity dates. For instance, if you have $5,000 to invest, you should buy:

a one-year GIC for $1,000;

a two-year GIC for $1,000;

a three-year GIC for $1,000;

a four-year GIC for $1,000; and

a five-year GIC for $1,000.

After the first year:

The one-year GIC will mature.

The two-year GIC will now have one year left until maturity.

The three-year GIC will now have two years left until maturity.

The four-year GIC will now have three years left until maturity.

The five-year GIC will now have four years left until maturity.

As your GIC matures each year, you should reinvest the proceeds in a new five-year GIC, to replace your most recent five-year GIC, which now has only four years left until it matures. (Whoa, boy. Say that again, five times, fast, with three slices of bread in your mouth, covered in peanut butter.)

Follow this strategy year after year. (You'll eat enough bread to cover Cleveland, and you'll weigh as much as the Brooklyn Bridge.) No matter what happens, one GIC will mature every year, and you'll continually reinvest the money at the current interest rate.

▲ Not Another Lesson: CSBs

Canada Savings Bonds (CSBs) are one of the most popular savings instruments. Each fall, CSBs are sold through financial institutions like banks and trust companies to Canadian residents in denominations of $100, $300, $500, $1,000, $5,000, and $10,000. Currently the limit on the total value of CSBs that you can purchase in one year is $100,000. (Sorry, Eugene.)

Purchasers can choose bonds that pay regular or compound interest. Interest rates for CSBs are set each year when they're issued, and are guaranteed for only one year. Each year, the CSB yield may stay the same or go up or down, depending upon the current economic climate.

> ### Facts for a Buck
>
> You can put Canada Savings Bonds in your RRSP at an interest rate that begins at 3.5% and rises over the next seven years to 6.5%. These interest rates may not seem high, but they're above the rate of inflation, and they're guaranteed. So go forth and make up your own mind.

Looney Lingo

REGULAR INTEREST BONDS pay you interest each November 1, either by cheque or by direct deposit to your account. COMPOUND INTEREST BONDS reinvest your interest automatically, so your savings continue to grow until the bonds are cashed or reach maturity.

Pros and Cons:

The advantages of CSBs are:

➤ They're easy to purchase;

LEARN AND EARN Do not confuse CSBs with conventional government and corporate bonds. Although they're both called bonds, Canada Savings Bonds do not respond like conventional bonds to interest-rate swings. No matter how high or how low rates go, you can always cash in your Canada Savings Bond and get your full investment back, even if you cash it in before it matures. That's because the government guarantees the full value of CSBs. (We'll deal with conventional bonds in another chapter.)

Because there's so little risk associated with CSBs, no one pays a premium or a discount to buy them. The only risk associated with a CSB comes from inflation.

➤ They're extremely safe; and

➤ They're highly liquid (which means you can always find someone to take them off your hands if you want to cash them in).

The disadvantages of CSBs are:

➤ They must be held for at least three months before you can collect any accrued interest;

➤ When you go to roll over your CSB — that is, when your CSB matures after one year and you take the money, rolled up like a big snowball, and immediately buy another CSB, so that it picks up more money in interest, just like a snowball picks up more snow and gets bigger and bigger as you roll it over again and again — you can't predict the interest rate that will prevail at the time.

Looney Lingo

We use the word LIQUID to describe investments that you can convert easily into cash.

▲ Last Lesson, I Promise: Mortgage-Backed Securities

Mortgage-backed securities (MBSs) are pools of high-grade residential mortgages. They work like this: Financial institutions put together hundreds of mortgages into a single package, called a pool. Then they sell shares in the pool to investors like you. Theoretically, you're lending your money to a borrower whose mortgage is in the pool. The financial institution is acting as an intermediary.

Each pool comes with its own interest rate and payment schedule. If a mortgage borrower defaults on a mortgage in the pool, you don't lose your money. That's because the interest and principal of the mortgage are both guaranteed by the Canada Mortgage and Housing Corporation (CMHC).

Theoretically, there's a correlation between the dollars lent in the form of mortgages and the dollars borrowed from investors in MBSs. But who really cares about that?

All we care about is the potential risk and reward of investing in an MBS. An investment in an MBS:

➤ pays an above-average yield;

➤ provides regular cash flow;

➤ is government-guaranteed; and

➤ is guaranteed regardless of the amount contributed.

What's in a Name?

In the United States, MBSs are called "Freddie Mac," "Fannie Mae," and "Ginnie Mae." In Canada, they're just called MBSs.

How Much?

You'll need at least $5,000 to purchase an MBS. MBSs can be purchased from brokers, and are issued by banks and trust companies that hold mortgages. Most are issued with five-year terms and can be held in an RRSP or an RRIF.

High Interest

The interest rate that you receive from an MBS depends upon the interest charged to the mortgage holders. The financial institution calculates the lowest mortgage rate of all the mortgages in the pool. Then it pays MBS investors one half point below the lowest rate.

Can I Sell My MBS Before It Matures?

If you want to cash in your MBS before it matures, you'll have to sell it to somebody else. However, that's not a problem. A lot of people buy and sell MBSs. They form a market, called a secondary market.

However, if you sell the MBS before it matures, the amount you receive depends on the current interest rate. (We'll discuss this in more detail later, in the chapter on bonds.) When interest rates rise, your MBS will fall in value; when interest rates fall, your MBS will rise in value.

When Is the Best Time to Buy an MBS?

The best time to buy an MBS is when interest rates are high and beginning to fall. That way, you can sell it before it matures for a profit on your original investment. However, if you plan on holding your MBS until it matures, anytime is a good time to purchase one.

Read It and Reap

➤ Use a savings account only as a temporary storage place for your money, not as an investment.

➤ If you withdraw money regularly from your savings account, consider opening a daily interest savings account so your money earns interest from the first day it's deposited.

➤ Financial institutions insured by the CDIC will guarantee your money on deposit to a limit of $60,000 per institution, not per branch.

➤ Keep between 10% and 50% of your investments in cash, so you can pay for bargains when they appear.

➤ Deposit accounts pay top interest on balances that meet minimum deposit requirements, usually $25,000. Unfortunately, your annual rate of return is usually not guaranteed.

➤ Term deposits are short-term investment contracts that usually mature in 30 days to one year.

➤ Guaranteed investment certificates are investment contracts that usually mature in one to five years and usually pay a higher yield than term-deposits, but carry stricter rules about cashing them in early.

➤ Canada Savings Bonds (regular interest) pay you interest directly each November 1.

➤ Canada Savings Bonds (compound interest) re-invest your interest automatically.

➤ Mortgage-backed securities are pools of high-quality residential mortgages, guaranteed by the Canada Mortgage and Housing Corporation.

Chapter 4

Stocks: Stock Answers

> **In This Chapter**
> ➤ What are stocks, and why should we buy them?
> ➤ Why do companies issue stock?
> ➤ What are dividends?
> ➤ How to read the stock tables
> ➤ Selling short

Let's Take Stock

If you own a share of a company's stock, you own a part of the company. There are basically two types of stocks: common stocks and preferred stocks.

Looney Lingo

COMMON STOCK represents part-ownership in a company. As a share-holder, the investor can participate in the company's growth by electing its board of directors, voting on corporate policies, and attending its annual meetings.

PREFERRED STOCK also represents part ownership, but investors in preferred shares participate in the company's growth in only a limited way. For example, owners of preferred shares often cannot vote on corporate policies.

How Common Are They?

Thousands of companies would like nothing more than to have you as a part owner. You don't need a college education. You don't need any special job skills. You don't have to be an upper-middle-class male graduate of an established prep school or the daughter of the president. You don't even need a resume. You just need to buy some of these companies' common shares.

Think of a company's stock as a big piece of pie. If the pie represents the total amount of a company's stock, then each slice represents a share. The more common stock you own, the larger your slab of pie. It's up to you to find out whether the pie is filled with apple, cherry, lemon, or just crust.

LEARN AND EARN

Companies that sell shares of their stock to the public are called public companies. Any idiot can walk off the street and buy a share of a public company. And many do. These companies have to follow a lot of strict rules set down by serious-minded guys in suits about a century ago. The rules, such as publishing an annual report, reporting insider trades, etc., are designed to prevent companies from taking the public's money, then packing up and moving to Panama.

Private companies can sell shares as well, but they can't sell them to the general public. So if you buy a share of a private company, you might have a hard time finding anyone else who will buy it from you.

The shares of public companies are traded all day, five days a week, in public markets called stock exchanges. If private companies try to trade their shares on a public stock market, people call them ugly names and throw tomatoes at them.

Uncle Harry Inc.

Say your weird Uncle Harry wants to start his own company, Acme Buggy Whips. His market research has shown that buggies are making a comeback. Harry's all set to capitalize on this up-and-coming market. However, he lacks one important start-up ingredient: money.

Uncle Harry needs at least $10,000 to pay the rent, buy the equipment and pay the staff to get the business up and running. He tries the bank, but the bank lends money only to people who don't need it.

So Uncle Harry decides to sell shares in Acme Buggy Whips. After jumping through a lot of hoops that we won't describe here, he ends up running a public company, which can sell shares to the public.

He charges $10 a share. That price — $10 — is called the **par value**. (You don't really have to know this stuff, but it helps if you want to impress the bartenders on Bay Street.)

To raise $10,000, Uncle Harry has to sell 1,000 shares. The number of

DOLLARS AND SENSE
$ ¢ $ ¢ $ ¢ $ ¢

In Canada, there are three major stock exchanges, where stocks are bought and sold publicly.

- The Toronto Stock Exchange (TSE) is the largest and best known.
- The Montreal Exchange (ME) is a big player in certain areas.
- The Vancouver Stock Exchange (VSE) specializes in low-priced, more speculative stocks, including a lot of mining stocks.

There's also a stock exchange in Alberta called the Alberta Exchange (How'd they ever think of that?) and a commodities exchange in Winnipeg.

shares that a company issues is referred to as the **shares outstanding**. (You'll knock 'em dead if you drop this little doozer into a conversation.)

An inj48vestor who buys one of Acme's 1,000 outstanding shares will own 1/1,000 of the company. (Not much here to talk about. Maybe you should buy a nice pair of socks instead.)

A Piece of the Action

As proof of ownership, Uncle Harry gives each stockholder a certificate that shows how many shares he or she owns in Acme. A brokerage firm will usually hold the certificates for safekeeping. But investors can ask for the certificate to be sent to them directly.

Board Stiffs

The stockholders are responsible for electing a company's board of directors. The board oversees the operations of the company. They approve the hiring and firing of the company's top executives. They approve or disapprove if the company's managers want to buy another company or sell a piece of the existing business. They might approve or disapprove if the receptionist wears boxer shorts on his head, but there's not much they can do about it. That's up to the people they appoint to run the company, like the president, the chief executive officer, and other guys with fancy titles. They don't do windows.

Once a year, the company holds a stockholders' meeting, where it provides investors with its annual report. This report contains two important pieces of information: the balance sheet and the statement of income.

If investors are dissatisfied with the way the company is being run, they can say so at the meeting. For every share owned, the stockholder gets one vote. The more shares owned, the more votes the stockholder gets.

Looney Lingo

The BALANCE SHEET shows what the company owns (assets) and owes (liabilities). It also shows the value of all the shares owned by the company's shareholders and the value per share.

The STATEMENT OF INCOME is a record of the company's sales, costs, and profits for the year.

The rest of the annual report is full of pretty pictures and long boring sentences. All this malarkey is window dressing. It wins awards from The Financial Post, *but it's not necessary for your investment decisions.*

Why Buy Stocks?

There is only one reason why anyone would invest in Acme Buggy Whips or any other company: money. You might think you're doing Uncle Harry a favour by buying shares in his company. But unless you think the company can make money, for you and Uncle Harry alike, you should save your money and tell Uncle Harry to get a real job.

Once you invest in a company's shares, how do you earn a profit? There are two ways:

➤ dividends or

➤ increases in the stock's value.

Dooby Dooby Dividend

After one year in business, Acme Buggy Whips has earned $1,000 in profits. With the approval of the board of directors, the company can either divide the $1,000 equally among the stockholders, in the form of dividends, or keep the profits and use the money to buy new machinery or expand the business.

With the board's approval, Acme Buggy Whips decides to put $500 back into the business. This $500 is called **retained earnings.** (More fodder for late-night conversations with your stockbroker.)

The company pays the remaining $500 to investors. Each shareholder receives 50¢ for every share owned. That 50¢ per share is calculated by dividing the total amount allotted to the company's dividend ($500) by the number of shares outstanding (1,000).

The Bottom Line Is More Than a New York Nightclub

Why do the prices of stocks go up and down like yo-yos? And why do people seem to care so much about the price of their shares?

The actual value of a stock is determined by the powers of supply and demand. A stock is worth only what somebody else is willing to pay for it. When 15 people all want to buy the stock and only one person wants to sell it, the stock price will rise. That's supply and demand. "You want it? Then pay me more for it than those other 14 people beside you will pay."

On the other side of the coin, when 15 people want to sell a stock and only one wants to buy, the stock price will fall until the buyer agrees with the price. "I won't pay you a penny more for that garbage."

But there's more to the story of a share's ups and downs. Buyers and sellers pay attention to corporate earnings, for example. If earnings rise steadily, so does the stock price. When earnings fall, the stock price generally falls too.

Just to make matters interesting, though, sometimes earnings go up as stock prices fall. Sometimes earnings will fall as stock prices go up. Who's driving this bus anyway?

If You Fell Asleep in Miss Dingleberry's Math Class, Skip This Example

For example, if a company has net earnings of $100 million, and it has 20 million shares outstanding, then the earnings per share are $5 ($100 million/20 million = $5).

True Value and How to Figure It Out

Here are two calculations to determine the value of a stock:

➤ the price/earnings ratio; and

➤ the dividend yield.

The Price/Earnings Ratio or If You Don't Have a Headache Yet, You Will

Also referred to as the P/E ratio or P/E multiple, the Price/Earnings ratio measures the current price of the share in relationship to the earnings per share. It is calculated by:

Investors look more closely at a company's earnings per share than at any other financial figure. Like Uncle Harry's buggy whip company, any business calculates its earnings per share by dividing the company's net earnings by the number of shares outstanding.

➤ dividing the current share price by the last 12 months' earnings per share.

Example

Try this on for size: If a company's stock is trading at $30 a share, and the company earns $2 a share, the P/E ratio would be 15. That's because $30/$2 = 15.

So What?

The ratio of price to earnings indicates the premium that an investor will pay to own a piece of the company. A P/E ratio of 15 indicates that an investor will pay 15 times as much as the company earns in a year to own a share. Investors figure the company will grow and that they will recover their investment in less than 15 years.

So What Else?

The P/E ratio tells us how much the stock could potentially grow. The higher a company's potential for growth, the more value the market places on its stock. A P/E ratio of 20 indicates that investors will pay the equivalent of 20 years of profits for the stock. A P/E ratio of 40 means the market is much more optimistic about the company's growth prospects and will pay the equivalent of 40 years of profits for a share.

The market doesn't expect to wait for 40 years to get its money back. It expects the company to grow so quickly that it will recover its investment in a much shorter time.

Sometimes the market is right. Sometimes it's not.

More P/E

A low P/E ratio implies that a company has low potential for growth. It also tells us how much risk is associated with the stock.

The market may not expect much growth from a company whose stock has a low P/E ratio. But it also doesn't see much risk in investing in the company. So its stock price will remain relatively stable.

DOLLARS AND SENSE
$ ¢ $ ¢ $ ¢

When the stock market turns down, the stocks that decline furthest in price are the ones with high P/E ratios. As a general rule, stocks that have a P/E ratio above 30 represent a higher risk.

Warning!

A large decline in the P/E ratio of a company's stock is a warning sign. It indicates that all may not be well with the company. For example, if a stock's P/E ratio falls from 30 to 20 in less than a year, investors have lost confidence in the stock.

And Now, the Moment We've All Been Waiting For... the Dividend Yield!!!!!

Say this: "A stock's indicated dividend for the next 12 months divided by the current share price."

Now say this: "Dividend yield."

They both mean the same thing. But one's easier to say.

The dividend yield indicates the annual return that an investor receives from a stock's dividends. It lets you compare the annual return on different kinds of investments.

The yield from your savings account may be 3%, for example. The dividend yield from your shares in Uncle Harry's buggy whip company (not him again!) might be 2.5%. However, as we'll see, yield isn't everything.

LEARN AND EARN

Generally speaking, the higher the dividend yield, the better the value. However, you have to consider other factors:

- Is the dividend payout secure? (A company that's not in business doesn't pay dividends.)
- Is it likely to be increased in the future?
- What proportion of profits are paid out in dividends, and what proportion are re-invested in the company?

More of Miss Dingleberry's Math Problems

If a company pays its stockholders a cash dividend of 50¢, and the share price is currently $20, then the dividend yield will be 2.5%. Why?

Watch this: $\dfrac{\$.50 \times 100}{20} = 2.5\%$

Aren't you glad you asked?

Nugget of Wisdom

Some people invest in safe secure companies whose stock has a low P/E ratio but a relatively high dividend yield. These companies may not grow quickly, nor will they go down the tubes next week.

Other people invest in more risky stocks with high P/E ratios but low dividend yields. These companies may grow so fast that their stock will double in value overnight. Or they may go, "Ffffft ...."

High Interest

A company that passes all its profits to shareholders in the form of high dividends may not last long. To compete with other companies, a business has to re-invest at least some of its profits in buildings, equipment, employees, and expansion plans. It can't give all its profits to its shareholders.

Facts for a Buck

Anyone who thinks profit is a dirty word should talk to someone who works for a company that doesn't make a profit.

When a company earns enormous profits, it doesn't mean that all the employees run out and buy Cadillacs. Much of the profit is re-invested in the company, so that elevators will continue to work next year, for example, or the machines will continue to function well enough for the company to earn a profit again next year. The rest of the profit is distributed to the shareholders, who risked their money by investing in the company in the first place.

The Return of the P/E Ratio

The P/E ratio and dividend yield fluctuate constantly.

➤ When the stock price rises, the P/E ratio rises, but the dividend yield falls. Miss Dingleberry says, "Figure it out, dummy. As the price (that's the P in P/E ratio) goes up, then there's more P to be divided by E. The dividend yield — the dividend divided by the share price (Ol' Mr. P again) — works the opposite way. This time, the P is on the bottom of the equation. The bigger the P is, the fewer times it goes into the dividend, and the lower the resulting percentage." Or you can just take my word for it.

P/E Ratio: The Sequel

➤ When the stock price falls, the P/E ratio falls, but the dividend rises. (See Miss Dingleberry's comments above. Or just trust me. It's true.)

Son of P/E Ratio

Both the P/E ratio and dividend yield are influenced by increases or decreases in the company's earnings and dividends. Hard to believe, I know, but it's true, as well.

Heeeeeere's Harry!

If Uncle Harry's company goes out of business and he sells off all its assets — the plant, the equipment, those bodacious buggy whips — how much would the stock be worth? The answer is called the **book value.** (Bartender, another beer.)

Book Value: Not Just for Librarians

A company's book value is calculated by taking the value of all the company's assets, subtracting the liabilities and dividing that number by the number of shares outstanding. (Believe it or not, you can find all these figures in a company's annual report. Or ask Uncle Harry.)

But book value can be misleading. When a company has to liquidate its assets, it rarely receives full value for them. Nevertheless, stocks trading near their book value usually present good buying opportunities.

Name Your Preference

Even though they're bought and sold just like common shares, preferred shares are different in several significant ways. Let me tell you about those ways (pay attention, Edgar!):

➤ Preferred shares carry a fixed dividend rate that's higher than the common stock. (See Miss Dingleberry, above, to brush up on your dividend yields.)

➤ If the company that issues preferred shares goes belly-up, any money left after its creditors are paid must go to the preferred stockholders first, then to the common stockholders. That's why they're called preferred shares.

➤ Preferred shareholders often do not enjoy the same voting rights as common shareholders. But because they receive higher dividends, they're not supposed to care.

What's So Great About Preferreds?

Compared to common stock, preferred shares pay higher fixed yields. But their value is far less affected by a company's growth — or lack of it. So the preferred-share price is more influenced by prevailing interest rate trends than by the company's earnings. If you could get 6% on your money in a GIC and only 4% from a preferred share, where would you invest?

A company's earnings become a factor in the price of its preferred shares only if they fall to the point where they jeopardize dividend payments. Then all hell breaks loose. Crusty old geezers with cigars start sputtering and fuming. And the preferred share price drops like a stone.

At all other times, the price is based on interest rate trends. When interest rates rise, the price of preferred stocks fall. Similarly, when interest rates fall, preferred stocks rise.

Top Down, Sun Shining, Radio Blasting: Here Come the Convertibles

As with bonds, corporations issue preferred shares that holders can convert into regular shares. The holder of a convertible preferred share can convert it at any time into a specified number of common shares. Say a company sells its convertible preferred shares for $100 each. A conversion clause allows you to convert each convertible preferred share into 10 shares of the company's common stock at any time within the next five years.

At the time, its common stock is trading at $9 a share. Since 10 shares at $9 apiece are worth $90, there's no benefit in exercising the conversion clause at current prices, unless you really want to lose $10. But when the price of a common share rises above $10, then it makes sense to convert. For example, if the price of a common share rises to $12, you can convert your convertible preferred, for which you paid $100, into 10 common shares, and get $120.

Unlike regular preferreds, the convertible's price tends to move in line with the price of the common stock. This can be good or bad, depending upon which way the common stock moves.

Hot Tip

You should consider purchasing convertible preferred shares during periods of rising inflation.

Think of it this way: When inflation is low, the fixed payment that you receive from the dividend on your preferred share retains its value. But when inflation rises, it erodes the value of your dividend payment. If you convert the shares to common stock, the value of your shares may go up, and the money you make in the process won't be so vulnerable to the dastardly ravages of inflation. (For more on the dastardly ravages of inflation, see Chapter 10.)

High Interest

The best time to buy preferred stock is when interest rates have peaked and are beginning to decline. At that time, dividend payouts will be high, and stock prices low.

Two Nickels for a Dime

If shares are low in price, individual investors tend to buy more of them. When the price of the stock rises, individuals don't buy so many shares. For example, they'll buy 20 shares at $1 apiece. But they won't buy four shares at $5 apiece. Instead they'll buy only three, or even none at all.

So when a company's stock goes up in price, the company often splits its stock to lower the unit price. For example, if a stock appreciates from $20 to $60, the company might then consider a 2-for-1 stock split. At that point, each stockholder receives twice as many shares, each valued at $30.

A stock split increases the number of shares outstanding, while leaving unchanged their total value

The Magnificent 7, the Indy 500, and the TSE 300

Now that I have your attention, forget about those first two items and concentrate on the TSE 300.

Every day, news announcers on radio and TV refer to the TSE, which stands for the Toronto Stock Exchange. They may say it's up 10 points. Or they may say it's down 25 points. Whether it's up or down, do they really know what they're talking about?

In fact, they're talking about the Toronto Stock Exchange 300 Composite Index, also called the TSE 300. This index measures the general performance of the most important stock market in Canada. It's based on the value of 300 stocks trading on the Toronto Stock Exchange.

The index began in 1977, when the total value of all 300 stocks was $34 billion. Rather than juggle all those zeroes (sort of like juggling a billion politicians), the TSE allotted an

Facts for a Buck

The TSE index would have to rise 45 points for the value of those 300 companies to increase by 1%. But even if the TSE 300 rose by 45 points, it would not mean that the value of each of those 300 companies increased by 1% as well. Some may have gone up 2%. Others only 1/2%. And others may have lost 2%.

A market index represents a general market movement, not the movement of individual stocks.

arbitrary number of 1,000 to represent the value of the TSE 300 at that time. After that, every time the value of shares represented by the TSE 300 Composite Index rose $3.4 million from the previous day's value, the index itself rose by one point. So the news announcer would say, for example, that the TSE rose one point today, to 1,001.

Don't Have a Dow, Man!

The TSE 300 is the most popular market index in Canada. In the U.S., the most popular market index is the Dow Jones Industrial Average — the Dow.

Started by Charles H. Dow in 1896, the index originally included only 12 stocks. On the first day of trading, the Dow Industrials closed at 40.94. Today the Dow Industrials contain 30 stocks, and the index is currently around 4,000.

High Interest

Of the original 12 Dow Industrial stocks of 1896, only General Electric remains as a Dow stock today. The other 29 stocks include:

2) AT&T		16) Hewlett-Packard
3) Allied Signal		17) IBM
4) Alcoa		18) International Paper
5) American Express		19) Johnson & Johnson
6) Boeing		20) McDonald's
7) Caterpillar		21) Merck
8) Chevron		22) Minnesota Mining
9) Coca Cola		23) J.P. Morgan
10) Walt Disney		24) Philip Morris
11) Dupont		25) Procter & Gamble
12) Eastman Kodak		26) Sears
13) Exxon		27) Traveler's Group
14) General Motors		28) Union Carbide
15) Goodyear		29) United Technologies
		30) Wal-Mart Stores

Standard & Poor (Where Do They Get These Names Anyway?)

Some people think the Dow, with only 30 stocks, cannot possibly reflect accurately the activity of the entire U.S. stock market. For these non-believers, there's Standard & Poor's 500 Index — the S&P 500. It's based on the ups and downs of 500 large industrial stocks. And if that doesn't satisfy you, become a shepherd.

You Said It Now

In talking about the value of a share, a dollar is frequently referred to as a point, as in, "Acme shares rose 3 points today."

Say It Again, Sam

The dollar value of stock prices are quoted in fractions of $1/8$ or more. Each $1/8$ of a dollar equals 12.5¢. A stock quoted with a price of $12 1/4$ is worth $12.25. A stock selling at $12 7/8$ is selling for $12.88.

Gobbledygook or Gems of Wisdom?

Everything you need to know about a company's day-to-day financial performance you can find in the stock tables. You just have to know how to read all that gibberish. Here's how:

---

52 Weeks

Hi	Lo	Stock	Sym	Div	Yld %	Vol 100s	Hi	Lo	Close	Net Chg
50-$3/8$	42	BCE Inc	B	2.68	5.4	21680	50-$3/8$	49-$1/8$	50-$1/8$	+1-$1/8$

➤ Hi and Lo: These show the highest and the lowest price that the stock traded at over the previous 52 weeks.

➤ Stock: This is the name of the company whose stock you're looking at.

➤ Sym: This is the symbol that represents BCE's stock on the ticker. (You can see the ticker in action in brokerage offices.)

➤ Div: This is the company's estimated annual dividend per share.

➤ Yld %: This is the stock's dividend yield.

➤ Vol 100s: This is the number of shares that have been traded throughout the day.

➤ The last few columns represent the highest price throughout the day, the lowest price throughout the day, the closing price at the end of the day, and the percent of change from the previous day.

Bid and Ask

As with most things in life, the people who want to sell stock usually want more than anyone else will pay for it.

Likewise, as with most things in life, the people who want to buy stock usually want to pay less than anyone wants to sell it for.

Buyers bid; sellers ask.

Money Talks

Look at a few consecutive annual reports for BCE or go through back issues of a newspaper's stock pages. You'll see that BCE's expected dividend of $2.68 is 31¢ more than the $2.37 per share in 1986, and $1.49 more than the $1.19 dividend per share payment in 1976.

BCE stockholders have benefited over the years as earnings more than doubled, while the company's directors steadily increased the dividend payment. That helps to explain why BCE's share price has increased from $16.75 in 1982 to over $50 today.

Board Lots, Odd Lots, Thanks a Lot

When you go to the supermarket to buy eggs, you see a price listed for one dozen. When it comes to eggs, one dozen — 12 to its friends — is the standard unit.

When it comes to stocks, the standard unit is 100 shares. Just as 12 eggs are called a dozen, 100 shares are called a board lot. For stocks trading over $1, the bid and ask prices are quoted per board lot. A purchase of under 100 shares is known as an odd lot.

LEARN AND EARN

A stock may have an ask price of $10 and a bid of $9^3/_4$. If you wanted to sell the stock right away, you'd have to accept the bid price of $9.75. If you wanted to buy the stock right away, you'd have to pay the ask price of $10.

You can also place an order to buy or sell a stock at a price in between the bid and ask, at $9^7/_8$. But if you do, there's no guarantee that your order will get filled.

Bid and ask prices are constantly changing in relation to supply and demand.

Waiter, I'd Like to Order

All investors should know how to place an order properly with a stockbroker to buy or sell stocks. First, don't stick your fingers in your ears and wiggle them at the broker. He won't pay any attention to you.

Instead, tell him nicely that you want to place one of three main types of orders:

1. **A market order**: You want to buy a particular stock at the current market price. For example, let's say you want to buy 100 shares of BCE Inc. You would call up your stockbroker and say, "Hi Mom, what's BCE trading at?" She'll say, "50 bid, $50^1/_4$ ask." If you find this range attractive, you say, "Buy 100 shares of BCE at the market." Your broker will repeat the order to you and then place it. Bing, bang, bong... you now own 100 shares of BCE at $50^1/_4$.

2. **A limit order**: You want to buy or sell a stock only if it trades at a specified price. You also have to set a time limit for your order. You could set the time limit for one day, one month, or any duration in between. Or you could place an order "good till cancelled," in which case the order stays in effect until it's either executed or cancelled by you.

    For example, if BCE is trading at $50, but you don't want to pay more than $48 for it, you would tell your broker to "Buy BCE at $48, good for the week." At the end of one week, if the trade isn't executed, it's automatically cancelled.

3. **A stop order:** You want to sell a stock whose price has gone up

and is now starting to fall. So you instruct your broker: "Place a stop order! AAAAHHHHH!!!"

For example, if you bought a stock at $20, it rose to $40, and it's now starting to head lower — $39 ... $38 ... $37 ... you don't want to lose your profits. So you phone your broker and say, "Hi, Mom, place a stop order to sell 100 shares at $35. AAAAHHHHH!!!!!" Now if the stock drops to $35, your shares will automatically be sold.

Words of Wisdom

Companies typically report their earnings per share every three months. Each three-month period is referred to as a quarter. (This will come in handy in a moment. So pay attention and get your feet off the sofa, Edgar.)

How to Select Winning Stocks

The most important factor for picking a winning stock is an increase in the company's earnings per share.

Buy a stock only if it records an increase in earnings per share of at least 30% to 50% in the most recent quarter compared to the same quarter last year.

High Interest

Once the price of a stock increases by 40% to 50% profit on a stock, it's prudent to place a stop order at 5% below the stock's most recent high. This way you protect your profits.

DOLLARS AND SENSE

Over the long term, the average stock price rises by 10% to 12% a year. But the prices of individual stocks do not always follow that average. The price of a stock can fall so quickly, it will eliminate gains accumulated over the entire previous year.

With this in mind, you should not regard individual stocks as long-term investments. Instead, think of them as trading vehicles, like chestnuts, marbles, baseball cards, and Elvis Presley's underwear. Once you've made a substantial profit on a particular stock, sell it.

Here's another way to put it: A stock earned 30¢ a share in the quarter ending in March of the previous year. You should consider buying it only if, in the quarter ending in March of this year, it earns 39¢ or more per share. (Say that five times, fast. Now read it backwards.)

Golden Years

Yearly earnings are also very important. Top-performing stocks should have at least a four-year to five-year track record of back-to-back increases in annual earnings per share.

For example:

YEAR	1993	1994	1995	1996	1997
EARNINGS PER SHARE	$0.14	$0.34	$0.80	$1.29	$1.42

Industry Groups or What's Your Sign?

Compare two stocks with similar earnings. One is involved in a leading industry — electronics, for example. The other operates in a lagging industry — say, buggy whips. The stock of the company in the leading industry will beat the other hands down, every time.

High Interest

Of all the stocks listed on the TSE, 45% are sensitive to changes in interest rates. These include:

- banks
- utilities
- insurance companies and
- construction companies.

When interest rates fall, these interest-sensitive stocks tend to do well.

The other 55% are sensitive to the economy in general. As inflation comes alive, companies involved in:

- steel
- gold mining and
- forestry and lumber

become the new market leaders.

More Interesting Stuff

Lower interest rates encourage people to spend money. So when interest rates have been low and are starting to rise, good companies in the following sectors perform well:

- retail stores
- cosmetics
- restaurants and
- tobacco

Near the end of a cycle, when interest rates have peaked and are starting back down, companies perform well in sectors like:

- pharmaceuticals and
- chemicals.

Don't Look Back

Never invest using a rearview mirror. Last year's big sector seldom wins again this year.

Thar's Gold in Them Thar Hills

Here we are, prospecting in specific sectors for companies that will perform well. We start with sectors that have suffered badly over the past few years. Now they're just starting to turn around.

For example, in December, 1992, gold had been beaten down to a seven-year low. Even though no one was buying gold shares, we could have made a bundle if we'd moved against the crowd and bought shares in gold-mining companies. Over the next year, most gold stocks rose more than 80%. Today, they're back down again, lower than they were even in 1992. Are you willing to buy now and hang on till they rise again?

Is The Price of the Stock Important?

With stocks as with anything else in life, you get what you pay for. With this in mind, never buy penny stocks whose shares trade for less

High Interest

Some people believe that a stock that trades for less than $1 can double in value faster than a stock trading at $15 or $30. That's a big mistake. What causes a stock to double is money, and these days, the big money is coming from the institutional investors such as pension funds and mutual funds. These investors almost never buy penny stocks.

than $1, unless you're looking for nifty wallpaper for your spare bedroom.

Avoid Hot Tips Like the Plague

If something sounds too good to be true, it usually is. For moderate risk-takers like you and me and anyone else who reads books before making an investment, blue chip companies make the best investments. (But even they can stumble. General Motors has. So has IBM. See "Don't put all your eggs in one basket.")

Strategies

Look for profitable companies. Then check the stock tables. If they're trading at the low end of their spectrum, now's the time to buy. (Unfortunately, some may keep on going down. See "Don't put all your eggs in one basket.")

Bargains usually emerge when the whole stock market turns down about 5% or 10%. These short dips are known as corrections. They generally occur once or twice a year.

Bulls, Bears, Crabs — What Kind of Zoo Is This?

When a bull attacks a matador during a bullfight, he thrusts his horns upward. An upward thrust in the stock market is called a bull market. That's one explanation. Another is that bull markets resemble bulls charging full steam ahead. Take your pick. (Or make up your own. It's all bull anyway.)

A bear attacks by swinging his paw downward. A ferocious downward swing in stock prices is called a bear market. That's one theory. Here's another. In colonial America, grizzly old coots called bear jobbers used to find a buyer for a bearskin, collect the payment up front, then go out and shoot a bear and deliver the skin. This resembles the activity of a short seller. Short sellers borrow stock at a high price, sell it, and wait for the price to go down. Then they buy the shares back at a lower price, return them to their owners, and keep the difference in price. (You decide. Or make up your own if you can bear it.)

A crab market moves sideways. (This could go on forever. Anyone for tuna?)

Don't Put All Your Eggs in One Basket (You Knew It Was Coming)

About 75% of stocks follow the general stock market trend. The other 25% march to a different drummer. The challenge is to figure out which are which, so you can get in at the bottom and ride a stock to the top, rather than getting in at the bottom just as the bottom falls out.

That's why the "Don't-put-all-your-eggs-in-one-basket" theory comes in handy. This theory is also called asset allocation. (Now, I ask you, which one would you choose to explain your strategy to an attractive stranger?)

Asset allocation means you always put some of your money in cash (see Chapter 3), some in income-producing investments, and some in stocks or stock funds. If a bear market comes along, you can limit your losses. (See Chapter 13 on Investment Strategies.)

Facts for a Buck

In the 40 years between 1956 and 1996, there were 13 bull markets and 12 bear markets.

- The bull markets lasted 7 to 44 months.
- Each was followed by a bear market lasting between 2 and 36 months.
- The gains during the bull markets ranged from 22% to 150%.
- The losses during bear markets ranged from 16% to 45%.

Conclusion: Over time, the market gains more than it loses.

Don't Sell Yourself Short

An investor can profit if a stock rises in value. You can also profit if a stock declines in value.

When you buy a stock hoping that it will rise in value, you are said to be investing long. If you think the price of the stock will fall, you can sell short.

Instead of buying a stock and then selling it, short sellers sell a stock, then buy it back later, when the price is lower (they hope). They do this by borrowing stock through a brokerage firm, then selling it at the current market price. They wait for a while, biting their nails and eating Gelusil like ju-jubes. Then, if they've predicted correctly, they go out and repurchase the stock at a lower price. They return the shares to the original lender and keep the difference in price. Sometimes short sellers are wrong, and the stock's price rises. Then the short seller has to buy back the shares at a higher price, and suffer a loss.

Short Cuts

It's a lot easier to pick a stock that will rise than to find one that will decline. That's because the stock market, over time, goes upward, not downward. If you bet a stock will drop, the cards are automatically stacked against you.

Graphs for Laughs

Until now, we have focused on selecting stocks based on their fundamentals, such as earnings, P/E ratios, dividend yields, and book value. In stock talk, this is called fundamental analysis. (Sam, another round for my friends!)

Many investors base their investment decisions on the behaviour patterns of stock prices. Based on the ups and downs of a stock's price in the past, they try to predict the movement of the stock in the future. To do this, they use a lot of graphs that look like this:

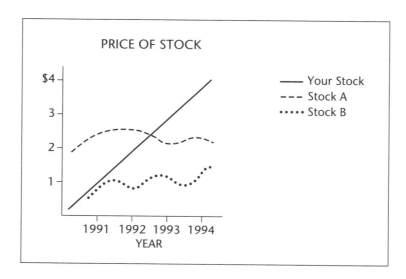

Sounds Foreign to Me

You can buy shares in foreign companies that don't list their shares on Canadian stock exchanges either by purchasing units of a mutual fund that invests in foreign companies or by purchasing American depository receipts (ADRs). ADRs are negotiable certificates issued by U.S. banks that represent the shares of a non-U.S. company on deposit with the bank's overseas custodian. You can't deduct the dividend tax credit on ADRs, and you may also have to pay a withholding tax on the dividends.

But if you think the future prospects of Gucci shoes look good, call your broker and order Gucci's ADRs.

> **LEARN AND EARN**
>
> For quick access to information on stocks and financial data, check www.fin-info.com or www.investor-corner.com.

> **High Interest**
>
> Graphs say a lot about a stock's performance. But you have to understand the language. One investor's graph is another's Swahili jigsaw puzzle.

Read It and Reap

➤ Stocks represent part ownership in a company.

➤ You shouldn't invest more than 35% of your money in stocks.

➤ Corporate profits that are returned to investors are called dividends.

➤ Two of the best measures of a stock's true value are the Price/ Earnings ratio and the dividend yield.

➤ The three most important stock market orders are the market order, limit order, and stop order.

➤ Beginning investors should stick to the well-known blue-chip type companies.

➤ Never buy penny stocks.

➤ Never buy hot tips.

Chapter 5

Bonds: Bonds of Steel

When interest rates are high, stocks die. When interest rates are low, stocks grow. With a hey nonny nonny and a boogety shoop!

In This Chapter

➤ What's a bond?

➤ How are interest rates related to bonds?

➤ The different types of bonds

➤ The best time to buy bonds

➤ Bond mutual funds

What Are Bonds?

Quite simply, a bond is a loan. If you lend me $1,000 and I write a promissory note that explains when I will pay you back and what rate of interest I will pay, that note represents a bond.

Whenever you lend money, you must make sure not only that you get repaid, but also that you earn interest on your money.

Before people lend money in the form of bonds, they want some reassurance that the borrower can repay them. Only then do they proceed to lend the money. That's why bonds tend to be stable, conservative investments.

Looney Lingo

FACE VALUE, PAR VALUE, and PRINCIPAL AMOUNT all describe the amount of the loan to be repaid. People say a bond has a face value of $1,000, for example.

The COUPON RATE is the rate of interest paid annually on a bond.

The MATURITY DATE is the date when the bond matures and you receive your loan back.

Who Sells Bonds?

Bonds are sold by governments and corporations. They're big, stable, conservative, and reliable, and they usually repay their debts.

When you lend money to the government, you receive a government bond. When you lend money to a corporation, you receive a corporate bond. The bond says the government or corporation will repay you, with interest.

Usually the interest is paid twice a year, at a fixed rate. On the date when the entire amount has to be repaid — called the maturity date — you will receive the bond's face value.

The performance of the bond market is closely tied to movements in interest rates.

Looney Lingo

In bond talk, the word COUPON means interest payment.

All You Ever Wanted to Know About Coupons

A bond consists of two parts:

➤ a piece of paper, which is the actual bond (also called the residual);

➤ a number of smaller pieces of paper, called coupons.

At one time, almost all bond certificates came with coupons attached. To collect your interest, you just cut off a coupon and cashed it in every six months or so. Rich people with whacking wads of bonds in their bedside tables sat around all day clipping coupons. (What a way to live.)

A bond's annual interest rate is also called its coupon rate. In most cases, a bond's coupon rate is fixed for the duration of the term. (But just to complicate matters, some bonds are issued with variable rates.)

Put on a Happy Face

The standard price for an individual bond when it's first issued is $1,000. That's the bond's face value.

Once you pay for the bond, you can wait till it matures to get your $1,000 back. Or you can sell it to somebody else in the open market.

More Looney Lingo

AT PAR: If a bond trades at its face value, it trades at par.

PREMIUM: If a bond trades above its face value, it trades at a premium.

DISCOUNT: If a bond trades below its face value, it trades at a discount.

COUPON: The little piece of paper that's attached to the bond. It represents the bond's interest payments.

RESIDUAL: Another term for the value of the bond itself. The residual is the amount you'll receive when your loan is paid back.

Open Season

Once bonds start trading on the open market, their price is quoted at $1/10$ of their actual price.

For instance, if a bond sells at par for $1,000, then it will be listed in the newspaper as 100. If the bond sells at a premium for $1,200, then it will be listed as 120. If the bond sells at a discount for $850, then it will be listed as 85.

Ups and Downs and All Arounds

When interest rates rise, the price of bonds falls. When interest rates fall, the price of bonds rises.

More specifically, when the prime rate rises by 1%, bond prices fall about 10%. When the prime rate falls 1%, bond prices rise about 10%.

Here's Why...

In January 1997, a corporation issues a $1,000 bond that matures in 30 years with an interest rate of 10%. Having read this book, you decide to purchase it. (Meanwhile, other corporations are issuing bonds at similar rates for 20 years or 10 years or even 40 years. Keep this in mind when we reach the punch line of this narrative.)

Bonds are issued with maturity dates ranging from three months to 40 years.

Short-term bonds mature in two years or less.

Intermediate-term bonds mature in two to five years.

Long-term bonds mature in five years or more.

In doing so, you agree to lend to this corporation $1,000 of your hard-earned money. In return, the corporation will give you a nice little certificate. It also promises to pay you 10% a year on your $1,000 investment, for a total of 30 years. After 30 years — but not before — the corporation will pay you back your $1,000 in full.

Stay with Us, Jocko...

In the year 2007, 10 years after you buy the bond, you decide you no longer want to keep it. You have two choices:

1. You can take it back to the corporation and tell the receptionist at the front door that you've come to get your money back. She'll announce your arrival to everyone in the company. They'll rush down to the lobby to stand around and laugh at you for being so stupid. They'll say, "Come back in another 20 years, you wiener, when your bond matures."

2. You can take it to the bond market and sell it to somebody else.

...Okay, We're Coming to the Punch Line...

If it's 2007, your bond is now 10 years old. It's no longer a 30-year bond. It's now a 20-year bond.

You originally paid $1,000 for it. So you should be able to sell it for $1,000, right?

Well, not exactly. Because money is harder to borrow in the year 2007, companies are issuing 20-year bonds with an interest rate of 12%. And there you stand with a bond that matures in 20 years but pays only 10% in interest. (If you can get 12% a year for 20 years on one bond and only 10% on another, would you pay the same price for them? Wanna buy a bridge?)

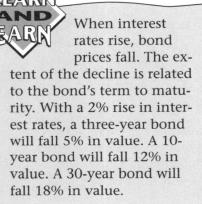

When interest rates rise, bond prices fall. The extent of the decline is related to the bond's term to maturity. With a 2% rise in interest rates, a three-year bond will fall 5% in value. A 10-year bond will fall 12% in value. A 30-year bond will fall 18% in value.

...We're Halfway There, Honest...

There's only one way out. You'll have to sell your bond for less than $1,000 to compensate the buyer for taking the crummy 10% interest rate. (In fact, you'll get about $830 for it. This price is based on a calculation involving the bond's net present value.)

...There. End of Story. No More. Finito. Over and Out

If interest rates have fallen to 8% in 2007, your bond will increase in value, because it pays 10%. With a smug look on your face, you can demand more than the bond's face value of $1,000. In fact, you can sell it for about $1,250.

Yield, You Scurvy Lout

When a bond is first issued, the yield is usually set at a fixed rate for the life of the bond. That fixed interest rate is based on prevailing economic conditions.

Once a bond starts trading on the open market, its current yield is constantly adjusted to keep it competitive with other bonds.

Even More Looney Lingo

The current yield is the actual rate of return on a bond purchased in the open market. It is calculated by dividing the bond's coupon rate by the bond's current price. For example:

➤ *When sold at par, a bond with a face value of $1,000 that pays a*

*coupon rate of 8% ($80) will provide a current yield of $80/$1000 =
8%.*

➤ *If the bond's price rises to $1,100, its current yield will be $80/$1,100 =
7.3%.*

➤ *If the bond's price falls to $900, its current yield will be $80/$900 =
8.8%.*

The Road to Damascus, the Towers of Babylon, the Yield to Maturity

If you buy a bond at a discount, you'll have a capital gain when the
bond matures and you collect its face value. The capital gain is equivalent to the difference between the price you pay for the bond and its
face value.

For instance, if you buy a bond with a face value of $1,000, and
you pay only $900, you will have a capital gain of $100 when the bond
matures.

The yield to maturity involves comparing the capital gain with the
years to maturity to arrive at the actual purchase price.

When you look at bond tables in the financial pages, the column
showing the yield represents the yield to maturity.

When a bond is purchased at a discount, the yield to maturity will
be higher than the current yield. When a bond is purchased at a premium, the yield to maturity will be less than the current yield.

Who's Calling?

Most bonds are issued with a provision known as a call. A call gives the
bond issuer the right to call in the bond before it matures.

This might happen if interest rates fall. Say a company issues
bonds in 1997 yielding 10%. In 1999, interest rates fall to 8%. If the corporation can call in its old 10% bonds and replace them with new 8%
bonds, it will save itself 2% in annual interest payments.

In return for calling the bond, the corporation will usually pay the
bondholder a premium above the bond's face value, usually equal to a
year's interest.

If you originally paid $1,000 for a bond paying 10%, the issuer would likely pay you about $1,100 to call it back before it matured.

Most bonds cannot be called in at least for the first five or six years after they're issued.

Give Them Credit

People who buy bonds like to know the risks involved. Is there a risk that the bond issuer will default on its payments? Will the bond issuer still be around when the time comes to cash in the bond?

To measure the risk of investing in a bond, investors rely on credit ratings. The credit rating of a company or government reflects its stability and trustworthiness. The higher the rating, the lower the risk and the safer the bond.

Federal government bonds usually have the highest rating. (Not always, though. If governments keep borrowing like there's no tomorrow, they end up owing so much money that they can't possibly pay it all back, and their ratings fall.)

Next in line are the provincial government bonds, followed by municipal and corporate bonds. The ratings range from triple A (the best) down to C.

Who Rates?

Bond rating services in Canada include Dominion Bond Rating Service (DBRS), Canadian Bond Rating Service (CBRS), Standard & Poor's and Moody's Investor Service. Your broker can tell you the rating for any bond that interests you.

Bond issuers pay interest for the privilege of borrowing your money and also to compensate you for your risk. The lower a bond's rating, the higher the interest paid by the issuer.

First in Line

A corporation is legally obligated to repay its loans from its bondholders whether it makes a profit or not. If it cannot meet its payments, the bondholders can force the firm into bankruptcy.

If bankruptcy occurs and the company sells off its assets, bond-holders must be paid first, before the holders of preferred or common stock.

Last to Profit

Unlike a shareholder, a company's bondholders do not share in the company's growth. They receive no dividends, and their capital gains are not related to the rise or fall of the company's stock price. Bondholders are loaners, not owners.

Ragtops and Convertibles

To make their bonds more attractive to investors, many corporations offer convertible bonds. These give the bondholders the privilege of converting their bonds into a specified number of the company's common shares at a specific conversion price.

These bonds still carry all the features of regular bonds, such as coupon rate, face value, maturity date, and call date. But because they're closely tied to the company's common stock, their price rises and falls in relation to the stock price. When the common stock rises in value, so does the price of the convertible bond.

The performance of these bonds is much more volatile than regular bonds. Convertibles also tend to carry lower yields than regular bonds.

Debentures (Not Dentures, Uncle Curtis)

Debentures are a type of bond issued frequently by large industrial corporations. They are not backed by real estate or property that can be sold to repay the bondholders if the company goes under. Instead, they're backed only by the general credit of the corporation.

First Mortgage Bonds

These bonds are backed by a first mortgage on the company's property. They offer investors first claim on the company's assets if it defaults on the repayment of its loan. They're generally quite safe.

Strips (Not Strip Poker, Uncle Len)

Uncertainty makes investors nervous. For example, they get nervous when they feel uncertain about the direction that interest rates will take.

Before you go to the bank or the trust company to re-invest a GIC or Canada Savings Bond that reaches maturity, you have no guarantee that the new interest rate will be as good as your current one.

One way to obtain such a guarantee is to buy a strip coupon bond. It will let you know exactly what you'll earn this year, next year, and every year until the bond matures.

OK, Unfasten Those Coupons and Strip

Say your typical long-term government bond has a face value of $100,000, a 20-year term to maturity, a 10% yield, and coupons that pay $500 in interest, every six months. Instead of selling these bonds intact, brokerage firms buy them and separate the coupons from the rest of the bond.

Now they can sell either the bond without the coupons or the coupons without the bond.

Do I Detect Interest?

If you buy a bond without the coupons, you won't earn any interest. To compensate the investor, strip coupon bonds sell at a discount. Instead of paying the full face value for a $100,000 bond, for example, you pay about $15,000.

When the stripped bond matures 20 years down the road, you can cash it in and collect the face value — $100,000. That's $85,000 more than you paid for it, which represents your earned interest.

The Advantages of a Strip Coupon Bond

➤ When rates are high, you can lock your money away to earn high yields year after year.

➤ Once you buy a strip, you can forget about it till it matures.

➤ No more worries about re-investing your money at lower rates.

➤ You're buying the bond at a discount, so you don't need a lot of money to invest up front.

➤ You know exactly how much money you'll have when the strip matures.

And Now, the Taxes (Did You Think You Wouldn't Have to Pay Any? Where Do You Think You Are? Bolivia?)

Even though you won't receive any money until the strip matures, Revenue Canada will tax you each year on the interest. That's why the best place to hold your strip bonds is inside a tax-free account such as an RRSP or RRIF. (We'll discuss these things later.)

Up Is Down, Down Is Up

The rules that apply to regular government bonds also apply to strip coupon bonds: When interest rates fall, strips rise in value. When interest rates rise, strips fall in value.

However, strip coupon bonds are about 60% more volatile than regular bonds to changes in interest rates. Say you invest $20,000 in a 20-year strip coupon bond when current rates are 8.5%. Then rates rise to 10.5%. Your strips will fall in value by about 25%. So you would lose about $5,000 if you suddenly had to cash in your strip before it matured.

Ordinary bonds that pay cash interest allow you to reinvest the interest at the new higher rates. Strip bonds offer no such luxury.

The reverse is also true. If rates fall, your strips will rise correspondingly in value.

The Long-term Scoop

Over the past seven decades, bonds have returned average annual gains of less than 5%. Yet many investors still believe the best strategy is to hold on to their bonds until they mature, regardless of the direction of interest rates. After all, they reason, no matter which way interest rates go, they'll still continue to receive their interest payments. And when the bond matures, they'll get its full face value.

When interest rates are declining, that rationale makes sense. But when interest rates rise, bondholders lose. There's no doubt about it.

That's because they lose the opportunity to invest their money in new higher-yielding bonds.

In June 1977, the Canadian prime rate was 8.25%. By August 1981, just over four years later, the prime reached 22.75%. By April 1983, it was back down to 11%.

When interest rates fluctuate so widely, bond traders can easily earn double-digit returns. But when interest rates are low and relatively stable, single-digit returns are the best you can hope for.

When Is the Best Time to Buy Bonds?

Rising interest rates mean lower bond prices. Falling rates mean higher bond prices. So we should buy bonds when interest rates reach a peak and begin to decline. We should sell bonds when interest rates hit bottom and begin to rise.

Now all we have to do is accurately predict the future movement of interest rates.

Strategy

Never buy bonds unless interest rates are high. That's the cardinal rule of the bond market. As a general rule, when long-term Government of Canada bonds are yielding at least 10.5% and inflation is under 5% annually, it's safe to start putting some (15% to 20%) of your money into bonds or bond mutual funds.

Long-term Government of Canada bond yield statistics are available in most financial newspapers such as *The Financial Post*.

DOLLARS AND SENSE

The bond market is five times larger than the stock market. It's also a leading indicator of the stock market. That means it indicates the direction that the stock market will take.

At Your Age, Dearie, You Should Consider a Hairpiece

An effective way to decide how much of your portfolio to invest in bonds is to use your age as a guideline:

Age 34 or younger: 5% in bonds or bond funds

Age 35 to 49: 15% in bonds or bond funds

Age 49 and up: 30% in bonds or bond funds

Bond Funds

Rather than investing with the aim of increasing the value of their holdings, bond funds focus on income.

They usually invest in government, corporate, and strip coupon bonds.

Like individual bonds, bond mutual funds respond to interest

High Interest

During major stock and bond market advances, bond prices usually start rising first, followed by stocks. Similarly, at the end of an advancing market, bond prices usually begin declining, followed by stock prices.

Over the past 80 years, the bond market has always undergone a major downturn either before or at the same time as every major downturn in the stock market. At the end of each of the last six recessions, when the stock market reached bottom, bonds began rising an average of four months prior to stocks.

What ties the two markets together? Interest rates.

The very thought of rising interest rates sends shivers up the spines of many bondholders. Then as interest rates rise, people pull their money out of the stock market and put it into GICs and CDs yielding double-digit returns. Thus, when bonds turn, stocks follow the leader and turn, too.

rates. When interest rates rise, bond mutual funds fall in value. When interest rates fall, bond mutual funds rise in value.

An Exercise

The price fluctuations (volatility) of a particular bond fund is directly proportional to the average maturity of all the bonds held in the fund's portfolio.

The longer it takes for its bondholdings to mature, the more sensitive the bond fund will be to changes in interest rates.

In general, funds that invest primarily in long-term bonds (maturing in 20 to 25 years) will be more volatile than funds that invest primarily in intermediate-term bonds (maturing in five to 10 years).

A short-term bond fund that invests primarily in bonds maturing in one to three years will be the least volatile.

Foreign Bond Funds

The Canadian bond market represents only 4% of the world's government bond market. So if you're limiting your bond investments solely to Canada, you may be missing out.

➤ 1986: Japanese bonds earn 37%; Canadian bonds earned 13%.

➤ 1987: United Kingdom bonds earn 35%; Canadian bonds, 3%.

➤ 1988: Australian bonds earn 18%; Canadian bonds, 9%.

➤ 1989: Canadian bonds are the top performers, earning around 13%.

➤ 1990: United Kingdom bonds earn 23%; Canadian bonds, 20%.

➤ 1991: Australian bonds earn 23%; Canadian bonds, 20%.

Dollars to Drachma to Deutschmarks

Before you can purchase another country's bonds, you must convert your money into that country's currency.

For instance, if you want to purchase German bonds, you must first convert your Canadian dollars into German marks.

That doesn't guarantee a profit, even if you're right on your timing, and German bonds appreciate in value. The mark could fall in value faster than the Canadian dollar. So when you sell your German bonds for marks, and then use the marks to buy Canadian dollars, you end up with fewer dollars than you started with.

This is called currency risk.

Hedges. Big Scary Monster Hedges with Berries Dangling Between Their Branches

To counter currency risk, some global funds hedge their bets by buying less volatile currencies.

A fund manager purchasing German bonds, for example, would sell marks on the foreign exchange market and buy a currency that will not fall so much in value, such as the U.S. dollar. The result is a currency hedged German bond position.

This type of fund is much less volatile than a non-hedged bond fund. However, because of the hedging, their potential profits are lower than non-hedged funds.

I Won't Grow Up

Individual bonds carry only limited risk if you hold them until they mature.

Bond funds, however, never mature. As soon as some of the fund's bonds mature or the fund sells them, they are replaced with other bonds.

If interest rates rise, the fund can actually lose money.

High Interest

Never invest in bond mutual funds when interest rates are rising. And if you've already invested in a bond fund, sell.

The Road to Riches (Not to Be Confused with the Road to Maturity. We've Already Taken That Road. We're on Another Road Now. Pay Attention, Betty)

Foreign bond funds have a history of doing really well or really lousy, depending on foreign interest rates.

Beginning investors should stay away from non-hedged foreign bond funds and stick to hedged funds like the Global Strategy World Bond Fund.

You should limit your foreign bond investments to 5% to 10% of your portfolio.

Read It and Reap

➤ Bonds represent formal IOUs between the issuer and the lender. The issuer agrees to repay the lender, with interest, on a specified date in the future.

➤ Bondholders, unlike shareholders, do not participate in a company's profit growth.

➤ The bond price is usually set at $1,000 per bond.

➤ Bond prices and interest rates move in opposite directions. When interest rates go up, bond prices go down. When interest rates go down, bond prices go up.

➤ A bond's current yield can be calculated by dividing the bond's annual interest payment by the bond's price.

➤ The yield to maturity includes the annual interest gained or lost on the difference between the bond's purchase price and face value.

➤ Many bonds today are issued with a call provision, which allows the issuer to retire the bond before the maturity date.

➤ Bonds carry ratings that reflect their risk. The higher the rating, the safer the bond.

➤ Convertible bonds offer investors the privilege of converting their bonds into common stock at a specific conversion price.

➤ Strip coupon bonds do not pay interest and are therefore sold at a discount to the bond's face value. The difference between what you pay for the strip and what you receive when it matures represents your interest payment.

➤ Bonds have historically been a poor long-term investment, averaging under 5% annually.

➤ The best time to buy bonds is when interest rates have reached a peak and are just beginning to fall.

➤ Never buy bonds unless interest rates are high.

➤ Rather than investing with the aim of increasing the value of their holdings, bond funds focus on income.

➤ In general, funds that invest primarily in long-term bonds will be more volatile than funds that invest primarily in intermediate-term bonds.

Gold: Golden Opportunities

A Little Background

Gold has fascinated humankind for thousands of years. Historians believe that people used gold as far back as 9000 B.C.

More than 5,000 years ago, the Sumerians used gold to produce weaponry, jewelry, and religious artifacts. By 3000 B.C., gold had become a standard of exchange between nations.

The Egyptian pharaohs stored gold in the form of bars and wafers. Hieroglyphic paintings depict large vessels returning from foreign lands filled with gold treasures.

Why Not Wheat or Beans or Sand? Why Gold?

Before they used gold, people used to barter. One man had a club, and the other man had a spear, so they traded. As long as it was a mutually acceptable trade, everything worked out fine. But what happened if nobody wanted your club, or if everyone wanted two clubs for a spear, or 50? It's hard to cram all that lumber into your wallet.

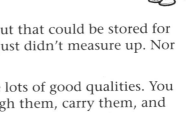

A more universally acceptable media of exchange had to be found. People could have used wheat. After all, everybody has to eat. But people wanted something that not only had wide acceptance, but that could be stored for long periods as well. In that regard, wheat just didn't measure up. Nor did ice cream.

So people turned to metals. They have lots of good qualities. You can cut them up and melt them down, weigh them, carry them, and store them. (Of course, you can say the same thing about tobacco. During the Second World War, cigarettes were highly valued and were often used as money.)

The more precious the metal, the better it serves as a medium of exchange. Handing a grocer 15 pounds of lead to pay for a quart of milk doesn't make much sense. Slapping down a gold coin on the counter has a lot more cachet.

Facts for a Buck

If you took all the gold that's ever been mined and assembled it in one place, it would fit inside a large warehouse.

More History You Don't Really Have to Read

Before there were gold coins, people had to measure the amount of gold they used for each transaction. If you bought a rug that cost a half ounce of gold, you would take out your gold pebbles, and the shopkeeper would weigh them for you.

In 550 B.C. King Croesus of Lydia had his image stamped on the first gold coins to authenticate their value. ("If it's Croesus, it has to be good!") Out went the scales.

If a pig cost a quarter ounce of gold, the customer just handed over two $\frac{1}{8}$ coins and took the pig home under his arm. Since the coins were stamped by a king, everybody felt reassured that the value of their coins was accurate.

So Long, Suckers

It didn't take long for people to realize that they could accumulate a tidy sum of gold by clipping the edges off their coins. They could still pass the coin along at its face value, while turning all those clippings into a big pile, which they could eventually sell.

Merchants soon caught on to this trick, and out came the scales again to weigh every coin.

To resolve this problem, all gold coins were issued with ridges around their edges. If somebody clipped an edge, the missing piece would be obvious. Back went the scales.

But it took more than a few ridges to stop some of the more determined criminals. Now they stashed a bunch of gold coins in a bag and shook the hell out of it. When the dust settled, so to speak, their profit lay on the bottom of the bag, ready to be swept up.

Today, our coins represent more value than they contain in metal. And they're made from all kinds of boring stuff like nickel and copper and even aluminum. But their edges are still ridged, just as they were when coins had some inherent value.

Another 196-Word History Lesson

When the Pilgrims landed at Plymouth, Massachusetts in 1620, gold was selling for $17.50 an ounce. A century and a half later, U.S. currency came into existence backed by both gold and silver in a 16 to 1 ratio. In other words, 16 ounces of silver was equal in value to one ounce of gold.

When gold was discovered on Indian land in 1835, an ounce of gold was worth $20.67. Gold rose to almost $40 an ounce during the Civil War, only to return back to $20.67 in 1880.

In 1900, the U.S. Congress passed the Gold Standard Act, which remained in place until 1934. That year, the gold standard was abolished, and the price of an ounce of gold was fixed at $35.

Between 1934 and 1974, it was illegal for U.S. citizens to own gold, except for the gold in coins. Then the law was changed, and any idiot could run out and buy an ounce of gold. And many did.

By 1980, gold was up to $850 an ounce. That was quite a feat. Only 12 years earlier it was trading at $38 an ounce. What happened?

Gimme, Gimme, Gimme...

The price of gold went up because people started buying it. Everyone — grandmothers, school teachers, nurses, writers of books about finance — bought gold.

As with most investments, when everybody starts jumping on the bandwagon, it's usually time to start jumping off. Sure enough, by 1982, the price of gold had fallen to US$325 an ounce. What happened?

Follow the Bouncing Ball

Realizing that the price of gold had hit a ridiculously high level, people began to sell and sell and sell. Gold stayed down at US$325 to US$350 an ounce for several months.

But near the end of 1982, another rally began. Over the next two years, the price of gold rose above US$500 an ounce, then floated downward, this time to less than US$300 an ounce.

Along came the bargain hunters again. (What do these guys do in their spare time?) Back went the price of gold, above US$500 in 1988. You're probably wondering what happened next. The price dropped as people sold. Gold hit bottom in December 1992 at around US$323 an ounce, rose again to close to $400, then plunged back down again to around US$310. At the time of writing, in late 1997, it's at US$311.

So What's It All Mean, Captain Mike?

Inflation occurs when prices go up and the purchasing power of your money falls. To avoid being stuck with piles of increasingly worthless cash, which has no more value than the paper it's made from, people purchase gold. Unlike cash, gold has value. Of that, you can be certain.

In fact, gold acts as a hedge against future uncertainty. When people don't know what to expect, they buy gold. In times of inflation, people don't know what to expect. That's why gold tends to perform best during periods of rapidly rising inflation. Likewise, gold prices usually fall as inflation declines. With gold prices as low as they've been in the last 10 years, speculators obviously think inflation is unlikely in the next few years.

Gold Is a Leader, Not a Follower

However, gold seems to move with a will of its own. When inflation seems low and under control, the price of gold will start to edge upward. When the rate of inflation is soaring and seems unlikely to stop rising, gold starts to fall in price.

If you look at the rise and fall of gold prices over the last few decades, you'll find that gold prices move ahead of inflation by 8 to 12 months. In 1980, for example, gold began falling from over $850 an ounce. Inflation was in the double digits and took two more years to fall.

It happened again in 1985. Gold prices started going up a year before inflation began rising. Gold prices rose again in 1993, while inflation was averaging only 3% annually. Now prices are back down. Will inflation follow, or is this a temporary lull?

Politics, Scandal, and Gold: The Untold Story

Political turmoil does not cause serious movements in the price of gold. Wars, assassinations, and constitutional jabbering may provide a temporary boost to the price of gold. But those movements are not significant.

For example, many believed that Russia's invasion of Afghanistan in 1979 was a major influence on the price of gold. But gold had already started its major advance prior to the war. The invasion didn't start the gold rush, it just accelerated it.

Theoretically, wars in the Middle East should have an even greater impact on the price of gold because of the potential impact of rising oil prices. But during the Iran-Iraq war of 1981, gold was already overpriced at US$850 an ounce. Except for a few temporary rallies, the major trend for gold between 1981 and 1982 was down.

During the Gulf War of 1990, gold prices fell below US$370 an ounce because there was a bear market prevailing at the time.

Money Talks

When the Vietnam war ended in the early 1970s, refugees had only hours to gather their belongings before they were herded onto waiting ships and planes. The lucky ones scooped up their gold and took it with them. When they reached their destination, usually at a U.S. air base, they could easily convert their gold into U.S. cash.

Should I Always Own Some Gold in My Portfolio?

Over the long term, gold moves with the rate of inflation. So its real value remains relatively constant. An ounce of gold today should buy the same amount of goods as it bought 100 years ago.

Compared to other investments, that's not a very impressive track record. Even if gold were to rise 10-fold to $4,000 an ounce, the price of most goods would also rise 10-fold.

Runaway inflation will never make gold owners rich. It will merely allow them to maintain their current purchasing power. These days, that's not enough. Investors want to beat inflation and make a profit, too. To do that with gold, you have to buy it when it's cheap and sell it when it's expensive.

A Tailor-made Strategy

To determine when gold is undervalued and cheap or when it is over-valued and expensive, I suggest measuring its price against a standard. Just as we know that $1 will buy a standard-sized 12-ounce bottle of Rootin'-Tootin' Root Beer, we also know that an ounce of gold usually buys a standard-sized good quality man's suit.

"A Man's Suit," You Say. "Gimme a Break. What Have You Been Smoking?"

You may laugh all you like. Go ahead. I'll laugh with you. Ho, ho, ho, ha, ha, ha. Now go and look in the window at that man's suit. How much does it cost? About US$500. Gold is at US$310. Is it a good buy today? According to our tailor-made theory, it is.

A good-quality man's suit is the one standard for measuring the value of gold that has stood the test of time. Sooner or later, the price of an ounce of gold always hovers around the point at which it will buy a good-quality man's suit.

At times, the tailor might give you some change in return for your ounce of gold. At other times, you might come up short of the full price (and the tailor will rip your sleeves off). But eventually, you'll be able to buy a suit with an ounce of gold, fair and square.

Gold and the U.S. Dollar

Another strategy frequently used is to buy gold when the U.S. dollar is weak compared to foreign currencies and sell gold when the U.S. dollar is strong. The rationale behind this strategy is that gold and the U.S. dollar usually move inversely.

That's because a strong U.S. dollar will help to push inflation lower. When the U.S. dollar is strong, it will buy more foreign goods. The threat of competition from cheap foreign imports forces U.S. manufacturers to keep a lid on their prices.

A weak U.S. dollar helps to push inflation higher. When the U.S. dollar is weak, foreign goods cost more, and U.S. manufacturers have more leeway to raise prices.

Since gold typically leads movements in inflation, the impact of the U.S. dollar can usually be first seen in the gold markets. A rising U.S. dollar will help push gold prices lower, while a falling U.S. dollar will help push gold higher.

Throughout the 1980s, the U.S. dollar and gold had a strong inverse relationship. Since 1990, the relationship has not been so strong, although the peaks and troughs have been closely correlated.

Gold or Gold Mines — Take Your Pick

Investors can either purchase gold itself, called bullion, or buy shares of the mining companies that produce the gold.

If you choose to buy gold bullion, you can buy it in the form of gold bars, gold coins, or gold certificates. Gold bars are the cheapest way to invest in gold. A bar can easily be converted into cash anywhere in the world. Also, its current price is widely quoted.

But if you want to keep it safe, you have to pay a storage charge. In addition, your money is tied up in an investment that is not earning any interest or dividends.

If you want to buy a gold bar, deal only with a reputable company that has been in business for a number of years. Make sure the bar is stamped with the purity, weight, identification number, and refiner's hallmark.

To purchase the gold bar, you'll have to pay a commission, known as a manufacturing charge. The larger the gold bar, the less the commission, relatively speaking. For example, one ounce of gold comes with a charge of US$6; 100 ounces carries a commission of US$100.

Flip a Coin

Many investors prefer to buy gold coins. The most popular include the Canadian Maple Leaf, South African Krugerrand, and the Mexican Onza.

Governments produce these gold coins not to circulate as currency but to make a profit from their sale by charging a premium. The premium usually ranges between 2% to 6%. When you go to resell your coin, you'll get little if any of your premium back.

Gold coins come in inexpensive denominations. If you can't afford to purchase a 1-ounce coin, you can also buy $1/2$-ounce, $1/4$-ounce, and $1/10$-ounce coins. They're easily convertible into cash worldwide, can be evaluated readily from widely quoted current prices, and can provide a profit if gold prices rise.

On the negative side, you have to consider the premiums paid, the storage risk, and the fact that your money will be tied up in an investment that's not earning any interest or dividends.

That Piece of Paper Is Worth Its Weight in Gold, and More

Gold bars and coins have to be stored safely. As a safer and less cumbersome alternative, you can buy a certificate. Instead of taking possession of the gold bar or coin, you buy a certificate registered in your name.

Similar to a stock certificate, it clearly states how much gold you own. It also gives you the right to demand payment in gold or its fair market value.

You still pay a small storage charge to the dealer for storing your gold, usually about $1/2$% of the current market value of your holdings. And you pay an initial transaction fee.

Most gold certificates sell for a minimum of $1,000. But they're by far the most popular method of owning gold.

Mine, All Mine

When gold prices are rising, you're usually better off owning gold mining stocks rather than the gold bullion itself. Want proof? Watch:

➤ Throughout 1987, gold appreciated by 40%; gold mining stocks rose 200%.

➤ Between September 1989 and January 1990, gold appreciated 16%; gold mining stocks rose 50%.

➤ Between December 1992 and January 1994, gold appreciated 24%; goldstocks, 100%. These days, gold mining shares aren't very popular, but they beat holding the real thing, by a long shot.

As I've mentioned, if you own gold bullion, you don't receive dividends or interest. You can only hope the price will rise so you can make a profit. (Of course, if you keep it in your shoe, you can always escape the country when the political doo-doo hits the fan. But that's another story.)

Many of the larger gold stocks, on the other hand, pay dividends in addition to offering a good chance of increasing in value.

Stock vs. Bullion: All Souped up with Nowhere to Go

Mining profits appreciate faster than the price of gold bullion. If a company can mine gold at a cost of $200 an ounce, for example, and gold is trading at $330 an ounce, the company can make a nice $130 profit. If the price of gold rises 20% ($66) to $396, mining profits increase by far more.

Oh No, Not Miss Dingleberry Again

Okay, kids, take out your calculators and repeat after me:

If the price of gold rises by $66, to $396 from $330, it rises by 20%. That's because $66 equals 20% of $330.

The same $66 increase in the price of gold has a far more dramatic effect on the profits of our gold mine. Its profits rise from $130 to $196, a whopping 51%.

Okay, kids, back on your heads.

A Poem, by M. Reardon

When stocks fall,
gold stands tall.

Thank you. Thank you very much.

> Before you run out and start buying gold mining stocks, you must make sure to check out the company that you're considering investing in. Many fly-by-night gold-mining companies are nothing more than a hole in the ground with a liar standing over it.

Dow I Godda Gold in My Node

Gold stocks usually perform quite well during major stock market declines. In fact, a strong inverse relationship seems to exist between the prices of gold and industrial stocks:

➤ For every 10% decline in the Dow Industrial average, gold stocks usually rise 5%.

➤ For every 10% advance in the Dow, gold stocks usually fall 5%.

Warning: usually, not always.

Make Mine Mutual

Instead of trying to pick gold stocks that will perform best, let the experts decide for you. You can do this by buying a ready-made, professionally managed, gold stock portfolio. This is called a gold mutual fund.

If you think gold is cheap and worth buying, a gold mutual fund is a hassle-free way to do it. Two of my favourites are the Dynamic Precious Metals Fund (1-800-268-8186) and the No-load Royal Trust Precious Metals Fund (1-800-463-FUND).

How Much Is Enough?

Some fans of gold recommend that investors always hold 20% to 30% of their portfolio in gold-related investments. Detractors go the opposite way and recommend never holding gold. Once again, the most prudent approach towards gold seems to be one of moderation.

A 5% to 10% portfolio position is prudent for most beginning investors. You should buy gradually, when prices are low, and then begin selling when inflationary pressures push the price of gold into overvalued territory.

Read It and Reap

➤ Gold has proven itself for thousands of years as the ideal medium of exchange.

➤ Over the past 30 years, the price of gold has traded as low as $35 an ounce and as high as $850 an ounce.

➤ When people fear rapidly rising inflation, they immediately turn to gold as a hedge against future uncertainty. As a result, gold tends to begin rising six to 12 months before inflation.

➤ The real value of gold has remained constant for hundreds, if not thousands of years. It will never make you rich, but it will maintain its purchasing power.

➤ When an ounce of gold isn't worth the price of a good-quality man's suit, it's cheap. When you can buy a man's suit with an ounce of gold and get change back from the tailor, gold is expensive.

➤ Ideally you should buy gold when it's cheap and sell it when it becomes expensive.

➤ You can ride the ups and downs of the gold market by buying gold bars, coins, certificates, stocks, or mutual funds. Most beginning investors should purchase gold through mutual funds.

Chapter 7

Mutual Funds: One for All & All for One

In This Chapter

➤ What are mutual funds?

➤ Open-ended vs. closed-ended

➤ Why should I buy one?

➤ Types of funds

➤ How do I buy one?

➤ Buying on margin

Have you ever wished that you could hire a professional money manager to watch over your money, who really knows the ins and outs of the investment world; who would make informed decisions about where to invest your money, and when; who could consistently earn for you 15% to 16% profit, year after year; and who, if your portfolio occasionally lost money, would earn it back for you?

That's essentially what you get by investing in a mutual fund.

Eggs in Many Baskets, etc.

One of the cardinal investment strategies for limiting stock market risk is known as diversification.

If you buy just one stock, such as IBM, and it goes down — or way down, as in IBM's case in the early 1990s — you'll lose money.

If you buy shares in 100 companies, there's a good chance that some of the stocks in the portfolio will lose money, while the others will make money. This is true even if you choose the companies in which to invest by sticking the newspaper's stock pages to the wall and throwing darts at them.

At the end of the day, week, month, quarter, or year, a single stock may have gone up or down. But the diversified portfolio will usually make a profit. That's the power of diversification. And that's what you get with a mutual fund.

Mutual Diversity

As individuals, few of us can afford to buy even one share of 100 companies. But as investors in a mutual fund, we can reap the benefits of diversity while sharing the costs.

The mutual fund will take your money and pool it together with money from many other investors. Along with their money, the mutual fund manager can invest in a broad range of stocks, bonds, or other instruments.

Voila! Instant diversity.

> **LEARN AND EARN**
>
> Mutual funds are professionally managed investment portfolios funded by thousands of people like you and me. But by putting even $1,000 in a mutual fund, we purchase the opportunity to participate in markets for stocks, bonds, and precious metals in Canada and in foreign countries.

Can I Trust These Mutual Guys?

In Canada, mutual fund companies must register with the provincial securities commission. In the U.S., mutual fund companies must register with the Securities and Exchange Commission. In either case, they're well-regulated, and their managers are well-qualified to make investments on their funds' behalf.

Banks Sell Them, but So Do Others

Major banks sell their own mutual funds. But many trust companies, insurance companies, and private companies sell mutual funds as well.

In fact, there are hundreds of private companies to choose from. They have names like Altamira, Trimark, Bolton Tremblay, AGF, Templeton, and 20/20.

Bay Street Blues

When deciding where to purchase a mutual fund, most people automatically head to their friendly neighbourhood bank and purchase the first mutual fund that the teller recommends. Don't fall into the trap. Make sure you check out all the choices before committing your hard-earned money.

DOLLARS AND SENSE
$¢$¢$¢$¢

Sorry, but you cannot buy one of the private companies' mutual funds (Templeton, Trimark etc.) at your local bank. Similarly, you cannot buy your favourite bank's mutual fund through a private company like Templeton or Trimark. They're all competing for your money. So compare them and choose the one that suits you.

Don't Worry, Be Happy

Investments in a mutual fund are not insured. But that shouldn't worry you too much. Here's why.

First, the big picture: In the course of Canadian history, no investor has ever lost money as a result of a mutual fund company going out of business.

"Yeah, but there's always a first time," you say. "So I should choose a bank's mutual fund, right?"

Not necessarily. Mutual funds sold through banks are no safer than mutual funds purchased from independent companies.

In any case, no matter who operates the fund, you won't lose your money if a mutual fund company goes out of business. You lose your money only if all the companies in which the mutual fund has invested go out of business. And if that happens, we might just as well start wearing bearskins and hunting for our next meal with a slingshot.

A Share Arrangement

Fund companies issue shares in return for your investment. The price of a mutual fund's shares varies from day to day. Some days it's a little higher, other days it's a little lower. Over the long term, however, the share price usually goes up. Some go up more than others.

Net Asset Value, or Do You Really Want to Read This Again?

The net asset value (NAV) is calculated dividing the mutual fund's total net assets by the total number of shares outstanding. If you read the chapter on stocks, you know this already.

The resulting figure is the price that you have to pay for one share in the mutual fund.

Alternatively, you could just look for the figure in the business section of your newspaper, under Mutual Funds.

The NAV fluctuates daily. Some days it may be up 5 cents; other days it may be down 10 cents. That's called volatility.

Up, Down, All Around

Stock prices of individual companies fluctuate in relation to supply and demand. When there are more buyers than sellers, the share price rises. When there are more sellers than buyers, the share price falls.

Same with mutual funds. When the stocks that make up the mutual fund rise in price, so too will the mutual fund's share price. When the stock prices fall, so will the mutual fund's.

An Open-ended Discussion

If you own shares in an open-ended mutual fund, you'll almost never have trouble finding someone to buy your shares or sell you more shares, at the current NAV. If investors don't want to deal with you, the fund itself will.

The most popular mutual funds today that are listed in the mutual-fund section of your daily newspaper are open-ended, such as Altamira, AGF, Trimark, Royal Trust, and so forth.

If It's Not Open, It Must Be Closed

Most mutual funds currently traded in Canada are open-ended. That's like saying most of the screws used in Canada are slot-headed. Then you find out that there are all those other screws with bigger slots and smaller slots, little square holes and big square holes, holes shaped like stars....

In keeping with the screw theory of life, there are also things called closed-end mutual funds. These funds issue a limited number of shares when they're first set up. Once they sell all the shares and there are none left to sell, the fund is closed. At that point, no new shares are issued, and the fund company will no longer redeem your shares.

That's where the stock exchange comes in. You can still buy and sell shares in a closed-end fund on the stock exchange. The price will fluctuate up and down, just like shares in other companies. Sometimes the price per share will be higher than the NAV — selling at a premium. Sometimes it will be less — selling at a discount.

Here's a Typical Listing of a Closed-end Fund

Fund Name	Stock exchange	NAV	Market price	Premium Discount
Korea Fund	NY	$10.14	$13.50	+33.1%

Here's What It All Means

➤ Shares in the Korea Fund are traded on the New York Stock Exchange.

➤ The current net asset value is $10.14.

➤ If this were an open-ended fund, you would pay just $10.14 a share. But this is a closed-ended fund. So you'll have to pay the market price: $13.50.

➤ Shares in the Korea Fund currently sell at a premium of 33.1% to its NAV. In other words, its $13.50-per-share price tag is 33.1%

more than the NAV of $10.14.

What a Load

Fund companies commonly charge a commission on the shares they sell. This commission is also called a load.

Contrary to popular opinion, they're not ripping you off by charging a commission. The commission simply compensates the fund company, financial planner, and stockbroker for providing you with a service. Your dentist doesn't work for nothing; neither do these people.

DOLLARS AND SENSE
$¢$¢$¢$¢$¢

Like the shares of other corporate stocks, shares in closed-end mutual funds rise and fall according to supply and demand. When more people want to buy than to sell the closed-end fund, the market price will rise above the NAV, and vice versa.

Looney Lingo

A LOAD is simply a commission that you sometimes have to pay when buying mutual fund shares.

Big Al's: Where the Price Is Right

Today, more than ever, competition between mutual funds is fierce. Every fund company wants you to invest your money with them. And

The Road to Riches

Never buy shares in a closed-end fund when they're first issued. Instead, you should wait until they first start trading on the stock exchange.

The reason? It costs money to pay legal fees and other expenses involved in arranging a share issue. So when their shares first begin trading on the stock exchange, closed-end funds usually sell at a discount to their NAV. This means the shares sell for less than the price at which they were first issued.

A prudent strategy is to wait for the fund to sell at a 20% to 30% discount to its NAV before you buy. Once they begin selling at a premium to their NAV, you should then consider selling your shares.

they've come up with innovative products to get you started at the least possible cost, such as:

Front-end Load: Cash on the Barrelhead

If you choose a front-end-load fund, you pay a commission ranging from 2% to 9% every time you buy shares.

LEARN AND EARN

A few financial wizards have discovered that instead of leaving your money in a mutual fund for years, you can make a higher return by moving your money every month into the previous month's 10 best-performing funds. If you have the inclination to do this, and you're prepared to pay the fees involved, you can beat the market return over a long period, these guys say. (So don't come back to me if it doesn't work. I'm just the messenger.)

Back-end Load: Baby, Please Don't Go

With a back-end-load fund, your entire initial investment goes into the mutual fund. You pay no direct sales commission up-front. But you have to leave your money in the fund for a minimum of five or six years. Otherwise you have to pay a commission when you remove it, called a back-end load.

The typical back-end-load fund charges a 6% commission in the first year, based on the value of your portfolio when you sell your shares; 5% in the second year; 4% after three years, and so on.

Most people should keep their money in a fund for at least five years anyway. So the back-end load won't affect you.

All in the Family

When the same company sells a number of different mutual funds, they're called a family. In many cases, you can transfer your money once or twice from one fund to another within the same family without paying a fee.

Go for Broke

You may wonder how your financial planner gets paid if you keep your money in a fund for six years and don't pay any commissions. (Or maybe you don't. I sure do. But that's because I'm a financial planner.)

The answer is that there are other fees involved in a mutual fund that the investor never sees. For the most part, these are the fund's management fees, skimmed off the top of the fund as it accumulates. The financial planner is paid from these fees at the outset.

These fees are explained in the fund's annual report.

No-Loads: The Free Lunch of Mutual Funds

There may be no such thing as a free lunch. But no-load mutual funds come pretty close.

With no-load funds, you don't have to pay a commission to buy or sell your shares. That's the good news.

But before you take your wad of bills down to the mutual fund store, wait till you hear the bad news. All mutual funds, including no-loads, pay their investment advisory team an annual management fee of between 0.2% to 2% of the fund's assets. This compensates them for making all the fund's investment decisions. Mutual funds also have to pay operating expenses to cover accounting costs, office rent, pencils, stick-em notes, and postage stamps.

These additional charges are deducted from the assets in the fund's portfolio.

The Road to Riches

No-load mutual funds do not provide the same quality of service as you'll receive from a professional financial planner or stockbroker. For instance, no-load fund companies will not tell you when to switch your money out of one fund that's underperforming the market and into another that's outperforming the market.

Nor will they recommend a competitor's fund, no matter how well it's performing.

An independent financial planner looks out for your best interests. He or she will help you find the fund that's best suited to your current needs and goals.

Beginning investors should think seriously about purchasing no-load funds only through an independent financial planner or stockbroker, rather than buying the shares directly from the fund company.

DOLLARS AND SENSE
$¢$¢$¢$¢ As a general rule, fund companies that sell front- and back-end-load funds do not sell no-load funds. Similarly, no-load fund companies do not usually sell mutual funds requiring a load.

All three types make money, providing you invest for the long term.

The Road to Riches

Investors who can wait patiently for five years or more to let their money grow should put 60% to 70% of their investments in equity funds. Over the long term, equity funds have outperformed all other investment vehicles.

Bay Street Blues

Investors who avoid mutual funds because they charge a commission are only cheating themselves. Don't think about commissions at all. Focus on performance and service.

Even if you have to pay a 5% to 9% commission, the potential gains of a good mutual fund over five to 10 years will make the commission pale by comparison.

Where Does the Dough Go, Joe?

1. Equity Funds

Equity funds invest in common stocks. They can be Canadian, American, or foreign.

Equity funds aim for long-term capital appreciation. That means they want the stocks held by the fund to increase in value over time.

If you're trying to double your money by next year so you can buy a new Porsche, forget about equity funds. If you're saving for retirement, then equity funds are your best bet.

There's More Than One Way to Skin an Equity

All equity funds invest in common stocks. But the similarities end there.

Some funds invest for value. They look for stocks that are priced cheaply relative to assets or earnings.

Others invest for growth. They don't look for stocks that are priced cheaply but that are issued by companies that are growing.

Other funds invest in a combination of the two.

There's more: Some equity funds invest strictly in smaller companies. Others stick with the big guys.

Big Things, Small Packages

If they grow at all, smaller companies tend to grow far more quickly than larger ones. A small company can take off on the strength of a single new product or service. The same new product or service will usually have only a modest impact on a larger company.

Small Is Beautiful, Sort of

Historically, the stocks of smaller companies have outperformed larger companies' stocks, but not always.

In 18 of the 23 years from 1960 to 1983, small-company stocks outperformed large-company stocks by a margin of almost six to one.

From 1984 to 1990, large-company stocks outperformed small-company stocks every year except 1988.

The past few years have favoured smaller company stocks.

You take your chances....

All mutual fund families offer investors a number of different types of mutual funds from which to choose. These include:

- equity funds
- specialty funds
- international funds
- bond funds
- income funds
- balanced funds and
- money market funds.

Go for Speed or Go for Distance

Many equity funds have established track records over the last one, five, and 10 years. Which one tells you more?

Conventional wisdom says you should look for good long-term track records and stay away from last year's hot funds. I have only one objection to that advice: It's wrong.

According to a study by *The Wall Street Journal*, last year's best-performing equity funds will still provide excellent returns this year. The funds with good five- or 10-year track records are usually not your best bet.

The study followed three investors:

➤ The first bought the top 25% of equity funds based on their performance over the past one year.

➤ The second bought the top 25% of equity funds based on their performance over the past five years.

➤ The third bought the top 25% of equity funds based on their performance over the past 10 years.

And the Winner Is...

The top-performing equity funds over 10 years earned average five-year gains of 82.6%.

The top-performing equity funds over five years earned average five-year gains of 80.7%.

The top-performing equity funds over one year earned average five-year gains of 95.6%.

Conclusion: When it comes to future five-year performance, the past one year is more important than the previous five- or 10-year periods.

Oh Tell Me, How Can This Be?

Some equity funds invest in growth stocks. Some invest in value stocks. Some invest in a combination. Growth and value stocks both tend to go through long periods when they're in or out of favour, and their prices rise and fall accordingly.

If you buy a stock fund with the best five- or 10-year track record, there's a good chance that it's about to go out of favour. On the other hand, last year's top-performing fund may just be coming into favour, and could likely be popular for some time to come.

The Road to Riches

Every three or four years, you should weed out the diversified equity funds that underperform the market and re-invest some of your money in funds that outperform the market. That way, some of your money will always go into the top-performing funds of the previous year.

2. Specialty Funds

Specialty funds invest in only one sector, such as gold funds, resource funds, or energy funds.

Important Announcement!!!!

Last year's hot specialty funds are often next year's big losers. Never buy last year's hot specialty funds just because they did well last year.

What's So Special?

Specialty funds do only as well as the sector they invest in. When they're hot, they sizzle. When they're not, they fizzle.

3. International Funds

A Looney Trip

Canada has the sixth-largest stock market in the world. But all the money that's invested on Canadian stock markets adds up to only 3% of the total amount available to companies throughout the world.

That means that if you limit your equity investments to Canada, you miss about 97% of the opportunities elsewhere in the world.

With this in mind, some mutual funds invest in stocks in other countries such as Japan, Britain, Germany, France, Italy, Mexico, and the Far East.

The Road to Riches

All investors should consider investing 10% to 20% of their portfolio in international equity mutual funds to diversify their risk and increase their gains.

Other countries often grow more quickly than Canada. When they do, companies in those countries reap higher profits. With higher profits come higher stock prices. If you invest in them, you win. Hubba hubba.

4. Bond Funds

Rather than investing with the aim of increasing the value of their holdings, bond funds focus on income.

They usually invest in government, corporate, and strip coupon bonds. (For more on these weird and wonderful creatures, see the chapter on bonds.)

Like individual bonds, bond mutual funds respond to interest rates. When interest rates rise, bond mutual funds fall in value. When interest rates fall, bond mutual funds rise in value.

Exercise for Big Brains

The price fluctuations (volatility) of a particular bond fund is directly proportional to the average maturity of all the bonds held in the fund's portfolio.

The longer it takes for its bondholdings to mature, the more sensitive the bond fund will be to changes in interest rates.

In general, funds that invest primarily in long-term bonds (maturing in 20 to 25 years) will be more volatile than funds that invest primarily in intermediate-term bonds (maturing in 5 to 10 years).

A short-term bond fund that invests primarily in bonds maturing in one to three years will be the least volatile.

OK. That's it. Hit the showers. Go soak your head.

Das Bond, La Bond, Bindi Bundi Bondi, etc. — Foreign Bond Funds

The Canadian bond market represents only 4% of the world's government bond market. So if you're limiting your bond investments solely to Canada, you may be missing out.

➤ 1986: Japanese bonds earn 37%; Canadian bonds earned 13%.

➤ 1987: United Kingdom bonds earn 35%; Canadian bonds, 3%.

➤ 1988: Australian bonds earn 18%; Canadian bonds, 9%.

➤ 1989: Canadian bonds are the top performers, earning around 13%.

➤ 1990: United Kingdom bonds earn 23%; Canadian bonds, 20%.

➤ 1991: Australian bonds earn 23%; Canadian bonds, 20%.

Dollars to Drachma to Deutschmarks

Before you can purchase another country's bonds, you must convert your money into that country's currency.

For instance, if you want to purchase German bonds, you must first convert your Canadian dollars into German marks.

That doesn't guarantee a profit, even if you're right on your timing, and German bonds appreciate in value. The mark could fall in value faster than the Canadian dollar. So when you sell your German bonds for marks, then use the marks to buy Canadian dollars, you end up with fewer dollars than you started with.

Yo, Where'd the Dough Go?

This is called currency risk.

Hedges: Not Garden Maintenance

To counter currency risk, some global funds hedge their bets by buying less volatile currencies. (They do all this internally, so you don't have to sear your brain by trying to figure out how many marks there are in a U.S. dollar or how many Mexican pesos you have to pay for an Italian lira.)

A fund manager purchasing German bonds, for example, would sell marks on the foreign exchange market and buy a currency that will not fall so much in value, such as the U.S. dollar. The result is a currency hedged German bond position.

This type of fund is much less volatile than a non-hedged bond fund. However, because of the hedging, their potential profits are lower than non-hedged funds.

I Won't Grow Up

Individual bonds carry only limited risk if you hold them until they mature. (If you're wondering why, go back and read the chapter on bonds.)

Bond funds, however, never mature. As soon as some of the fund's bonds mature or the fund sells them, they are replaced with other bonds.

If interest rates rise, the fund can actually lose money.

Reardon's Golden Rule #3

Never invest in bond mutual funds when interest rates are rising. And if you've already invested in a bond fund, sell.

5. Income Funds: Just Gimme Money

Income funds aim to produce income. What a surprise.

The Road to Riches

Foreign bond funds have a history of doing really well or really lousy, depending on foreign interest rates. (If you want to know more about that stuff, buy another book.)

Beginning investors should stay away from non-hedged foreign bond funds and stick to hedged funds like the Global Strategy World Bond Fund.

I recommend that you limit your foreign bond investments to 5% to 10% of your portfolio.

They do not aim for capital gains. That means they're not looking for their investments to increase substantially in value. They just want the investments to generate money in predictable amounts.

A large percentage of the money in such a fund is always invested in government and corporate bonds.

These funds are appropriate for investors who want income, but very little risk. People on pensions like them.

6. Balanced Funds: No Stunts for These Guys

Using a balanced investment approach, these funds invest in some stocks, some bonds, some gold, and some real estate.

All you have to do is sit back, relax, and let the fund manager maintain the balance. Boring, eh.

Over the long term, these funds usually generate lower returns than most equity funds.

These funds are for people who want to invest their money once and never think about it again.

However, investing once and forgetting about your money is not a strategy. It's a cop-out.

7. Money Market Funds: Put It in the Safe

Money market funds invest primarily in Treasury bills. You can't get much safer than that.

These funds almost always pay a higher rate of interest than a bank savings account, and all the interest earned will be converted into additional shares in your account.

As with all other mutual funds, your money is highly liquid. If you want to take your money back, you can usually have a cheque in your hands within 24 to 48 hours.

They offer an excellent place to store your money while you decide what to do with it over the long term.

T-Bills, Two Bills, Tea-for-two Bills

The Canadian government regularly needs to borrow enormous amounts of money for short periods. Once a week, it sells Treasury Bills in an auction to banks and other large financial institutions.

Treasury Bills are very short-term bonds. They mature in three months, six months, or one year.

T-Bills (as they're called by people in a hurry) are IOUs backed by the Canadian government. They're among the safest investments in the world. And there's a huge market for them, which makes them very easy to buy and sell.

Yabba Dabba Dividend

Like stocks, mutual funds pay dividends to their shareholders. They're paid on an annual, semi-annual, or quarterly basis.

You can choose to collect the dividend yourself. Or you can tell the fund administrators to use your dividends to buy more shares in the fund.

By the way, these dividends are eligible for the dividend tax credit. And if you know what that is, you should be writing this book.

Excuse Me, I'd Like to Buy a Mutual Fund

You can invest in a mutual fund directly. Or you can work with a financial planner. (I prefer the second alternative. Not because I'm a financial planner myself. Honest. I'm just trying to help you.)

If you go directly to the mutual fund — well, that's your choice — but don't say I didn't warn you.

A financial planner matches your needs and goals to the appropriate fund.

If you're single, make a lot of money, have few expenses, want immediate gratification, and don't mind taking a few risks, the planner will suggest an appropriate strategy.

If you're married with three kids, unemployed, paying off a mortgage, looking forward to your Aunt Beulah's arrival from Scotland to stay in your basement for the next 13 years, and would like to collect a pension income when she finally leaves, the planner will suggest another strategy. (Like, join an ashram.)

With the name of each fund that the planner recommends, you should also receive the fund's prospectus.

The Lone Investor

Standing alone, face against the wind, sun beating down on your head, you look with a steely gaze into your financial future. (Look, here comes Hoss.)

If you go it alone, you should call a number of fund companies — the more the better — and ask each of them for a prospectus. This is a booklet full of figures and tables that will tell you how and where the fund invests its money, and with what success.

You should feel comfortable with the fund's past performance, future outlook, fees, rules, and regulations before you commit any money.

Since you're making your own decisions, you will deal directly with the fund company or with a discount broker.

Prospecting the Prospectus

The mutual fund prospectus contains information about the fund: its investment strategy, its history, the fees it charges, rules for cashing in or moving your money, etc. It also contains an application form for prospective investors. It's put together by the fund company.

LEARN AND EARN

You can keep track of the performance of mutual funds over the Internet. At www.globefund.com, for example, and at www.quicken.ca, you can find charts, graphs, and information about fund characteristics and performance. Other good sources of information include:

Investorama	www.investorama.com
Thomson Information	www.marketedge.com
U.S. information	www.wallstreetcity.com

Unlike this wonderful book, the prospectus is usually written by lawyers, or people who'd like to be lawyers. They talk like this: In the event of the aforementioned eventuality transpiring before the expiry of the said termination clause, such clause will be deemed to have transpired before any expiry could be desired. With a boom-shakka-lakka-lakka-boom.

Go on. Read the thing. Then, if you have any questions, call a financial planner or the fund company itself. They'll be glad to help.

Other discount brokers include CT Market Partners (www.ctsecurities.com), operated by Canada Trust, and Hongkong Bank's Discount Trading Service (www.hkbc.com).

For information on mutual funds, try the Canadian Mutual Fund Portfolio Pages (www.pal.com).

Dis Guy, Discount Broker

Discount brokers charge less than a full-service broker to perform the same tasks. But they don't offer advice, and they don't really care if you make investments appropriate to your situation.

In other words, you're on your own, kid.

One of the best is Green Line Investor Services Inc. (1-800-268-8166) and Priority Brokerage (1-888-597-9999). Others include CIBC Investors Edge (1-800-567-EDGE) and E*Trade (1-888-TRADE-88).

When filling out an application form, make sure that you request telephone redemption and switching privileges. That way, you can move your money from one fund to another or remove your money completely with just a telephone call.

Also consider setting up an automatic investment plan. That way, your money will be withdrawn automatically from your bank account each month and transferred directly into the mutual fund of your choice.

You should also consider having all dividends and capital gains reinvested back into the fund. This will put as much money as possible to work for you in the fund.

A Few Good Funds

Altamira Equity Fund: an excellent no-load diversified equity fund.

➤ invests in small and large company stocks;

➤ aims for value and growth, so it invests in companies whose stocks are priced cheaply and also looks for companies with large growth potential;

➤ average annual gains between 1989 and 1993: over 30%;

➤ phone: 416-413-5359;

➤ write: Altamira Investment Services Inc., 250 Bloor St. East, Suite 200, Toronto, Ontario, M4W 1E6.

Templeton Growth Fund: an excellent load mutual fund

➤ buys bargains when nobody else wants them — straw hats in January;

➤ average annual return since 1956: over 15%;

➤ phone 1-800-387-0830.

Trimark Fund: one of the best international equity funds.

➤ average annual return since 1984: over 15%.

➤ phone: 1-800-387-9823 (Ontario & Quebec) or 1-800-387-9841 (elsewhere in Canada).

U.S. No Loads

In the U.S., there are more than 1,000 no-load mutual funds, many of which have excellent long-term track records over 15 to 20 years.

To purchase one of these U.S. mutual funds, just write or telephone the fund company. Many have toll-free 1-800 numbers, accessible from Canada. Ask for a prospectus, plus a W-8 tax form. (This form tells the U.S. Internal Revenue Service that you're not a U.S. resident and should not be subject to withholding of capital gains.)

According to Revenue Canada, your foreign capital gains still qualify for the $100,000 capital gains exemption.

The U.S. government will withhold some of your dividends. But you can get them back when you file your Canadian tax return.

Some U.S. mutual fund companies will not send a prospectus to Canadian residents. Big deal. Just open an account with a U.S. discount broker. That way, you can buy and sell any U.S. funds with a single phone call.

One of the best U.S. discount brokers is Muriel Siebert & Company, Inc., 885 Third Avenue, Suite 1720, New York, NY, 10022. (phone: 1-212-644-2400).

A Few Good U.S. Funds

No-load U.S. equity funds:

➤ Twentieth Century's Ultra Fund (write: Twentieth Century Investors, Inc., P.O. Box 419200, Kansas City, Missouri, 64141-6200; Phone 1-816-531-5575).

➤ The Berger 100 Fund (write: Berger Associates Inc., P.O. Box 5005, Denver, Colorado, 80217; phone: 1-800-551-5849 or 1-303-329-0200).

➤ The Kaufman Fund (write: Kaufman Fund Inc., 17 Battery Place, Suite 2624, New York, New York, 10004; phone: 1-800-321-9043 or 1-212-344-2661).

Margin: Another Word for Edge, as in Living On...

Margin is money that you borrow from your broker to buy investments. If you purchase $5,000 worth of a mutual fund or stocks through a brokerage firm, the firm will usually allow you to borrow another $5,000. So you can now buy $10,000 worth of shares, even though you have only $5,000.

The firm will insist that you maintain this 50% ratio of borrowed money to your own money.

Calling All Margins

Say you've bought $5,000 (50% of $10,000) worth of a mutual fund trading at a price of $6 per share. If the share price falls below $6, your broker will call you and ask you to put up more cash to maintain your 50% minimum margin requirement.

If you don't have enough money, you'll have to sell some of your shares to make up the difference.

My Favourite Margin

When the stock market is advancing, you can earn substantially higher profits by investing on margin.

For instance, if you have $5,000 to invest in a fund, and the fund goes up 25%, you make $1,250. But if you borrowed an additional $5,000 to buy $10,000 worth of the fund, you'd earn $2,500, even though only $5,000 of your original investment was yours.

You have to pay for the borrowed money, at a prevailing interest rate. But even then, you'd be ahead of the game.

My Not-so-favourite Margin

Sometimes the stock market declines. When it does, you'll lose even more if you invest on margin.

For example, if your stock or mutual fund falls 25% in value, from $10,000 to $7,500, you'll be down $2,500. That's one-quarter of your total investment, but one-half of your original $5,000. And you still have to pay interest on your $5,000 loan.

Read It and Reap

➤ Mutual funds are professionally managed investment portfolios that allow individual investors to put as little as $100 a month into stocks, bonds, gold, and real estate.

➤ Since mutual funds put their money in a variety of investments, your risk is substantially decreased.

➤ Open-end mutual funds will always sell you more shares in the fund or buy back the shares you already own.

➤ Closed-end funds no longer issue new shares or redeem your shares, so you have to buy and sell them on the stock market.

➤ Front-end loads charge you a commission up front. Back-end loads charge you a commission only if you redeem your shares early. No-load funds don't charge any commission to buy or sell your shares.

➤ Performance and service are more important than commissions.

➤ Beginning investors should buy mutual funds through a financial planner or full-service stockbroker.

➤ There are many different types of funds including equity, specialty, international, bond, income, balanced, and money market funds.

➤ When it comes to diversified equity funds, the past one year's performance is more important than the previous five- or 10-year periods.

➤ Mutual funds can be purchased through a financial planner, brokerage firm, or directly from the fund company.

➤ Canadian investors can open up a U.S. account and purchase mutual funds that are sold only in the United States.

➤ Investors who purchase their mutual fund shares through a brokerage firm can double their purchasing power by borrowing money from their broker. This borrowed money is known as margin.

➤ Always invest with your head, not over it!

Chapter 8

Real Estate: Home, Sweet Home

In This Chapter:

➤ Is it really the best investment?

➤ Real estate prices don't always go up

➤ What are the risks involved?

➤ Your home: investment or cost

➤ What to look for before buying

➤ When to buy

➤ Location, location, location

➤ Negotiating a good deal

Raise High the Roof Beam

Most people should try to own a house. It provides several advantages over most other investments:

➤ if the value of your house goes up, the money you make when you sell is tax-free;

➤ paying for a house forces you to save (nobody wants to lose his house to the bank);

➤ real estate has a good long-term track record; and

➤ you can live in your investment.

But Keep It in Perspective

Don't blow your whole bundle on a house. It's only one type of invest-ment. In fact, in many ways, it's not an investment at all. You should buy a house because you like it, because you can afford it, because your mate will leave you if you don't, because you're tired of sleeping under a picnic bench in the park, because you'd like to own something in 50 years, and for lots of other reasons. Only then should you buy a house because you think it will increase in value and allow you to cash in your chips and live happily ever after.

Wise Words (Listen Up, Pencil-Head)

You should be able to pay for a house and still invest in an RRSP, mutual funds, stocks, bonds, or at least a bus trip across the city. All but the last will come in handy on the journey toward financial independence.

A Pipe Dream

Ideally, the value of all your investments, including your house, will rise continually. When you decide to retire, each of your investments will have increased immensely in value. You will have lost money on none of them. You will retire with great wealth. The Queen will ask you to dinner, and I'm the King of Persia.

Ugly Reality

If you invest wisely, and the price of your house falls, the value of your other investments will compensate for the loss.

The Boom/Bust Cycle

Most of us have heard stories of skyrocketing real estate prices. And most of us think that house prices go continually upward.

For example: A house in Toronto that cost $10,000 to $12,000 in the 1950s is today worth well over $200,000.

But is real estate a good investment?

If you bought a house in Toronto in the 1950s and held on to it until 1989, you'd probably say yes.

You might answer differently, though, if you bought a house in 1989 and watched its price fall like a bag of nails from a 10th-storey window. By 1994, your house would have lost 10% to 20% of the price that you originally paid for it, and you still wouldn't have recovered the loss by 1997.

Money Talks

Although many people would like to see the 1980s repeat themselves, it's unlikely that real estate prices in Canada will increase at a rate much greater than inflation.

Investment or Cost

In the context of a financial plan, a house often becomes more of an expenditure than an investment. After all, you can't spend your living room. (On the other hand, you can't live in a stock certificate. But that's another story.)

Many of us think we'll eventually sell our house, move into a small condo, invest the money, and live off the interest. Unfortunately, few of us do that. Instead, we grow attached to our house. We like our neighbourhood. We like the redecorating that we did in the kitchen. We like getting up in the morning with the sun coming in the window to the right of the umbrella stand. Our kids come back to visit us. And we never want to leave.

Money Talks

As a rule of thumb, you should not spend more than 30% of your gross family income on mortgage payments, property taxes, and energy bills.

No Time for Bozos

You have to be financially and emotionally prepared for the potential risks and rewards of owning your own home. For example:

➤ The down payment on a house ties up $10,000, $20,000, or $30,000 of your money. In the 1990s, with real estate appreciating in value about as quickly as a 10-year-old jalopy, you might invest elsewhere for a better return.

➤ If you hold on to your house for 10 years or more, it will likely appreciate in value. (But if you bought a house in Chernobyl, the Love Canal, or Yugoslavia, you might be out of luck.) Are you prepared to hold on to your house that long? Or do you still feel like packing in your job and heading to Montana to live with the wild horses and Ralph Lauren?

➤ Can you risk taking a financial bath if you can't make the mortgage payments and have to sell your house?

➤ Can you afford to maintain your asset? A house takes tender loving care. Its roof can leak. Its basement can flood. Its lawn needs mowing. The driveway needs shoveling. But what else do you have to do with your time?

Will Renovating Increase the Value of My Home?

Some types of renovation will increase the value of your property. Others may not. You have to pick your spots.

➤ A renovated kitchen will usually pay for itself, unless you install solid gold faucets. So will a new or renovated bathroom.

➤ People love a cozy fireplace. Let them buy your house and find out that it's a good place to store the boots.

➤ An attic makes a great bedroom, and the value it adds to the house usually exceeds the cost.

➤ A garage adds $10,000 or more to the value of your house.

Other Boo-Boos of Remodeling

➤ Swimming pools: If you like to do the dog paddle in your own backyard, that's fine. But don't expect to add value to your house by building a pool. A lot of people, including families with small children, won't go near them.

➤ Air conditioning makes you sleep better at night. That's fine, too. But buyers won't line up at your door just because you installed central air last year.

➤ Hot tubs, fairy lights, plastic hydrangea bushes, and doorbells that play Inna-Gadda-Da-Vida are indulgences for your own weird and wonderful excesses. They're not investments in the value of your house.

Janis Joplin's Mortgage Blues: Carry That Ball and Chain

When interest rates are low, borrow as much money as you can to buy a house. That way, you'll get the highest return on your investment.

> **DOLLARS AND SENSE**
> $¢$¢$¢$¢
>
> The bigger the house, the better the investment. But don't buy more house than you can comfortably afford.

In fact, never pay cash for a house. Always use borrowed money, even if you have $200,000 in loonies burning a hole in your pocket. (And probably holding your pants down around your ankles, too.)

But Uncle Sylvester Says Only Louts and Goof-Offs Borrow Money If They Don't Have To

Tell Uncle Sylvester to go pound sand. Here's why:

Say you have $200,000 in cash. You buy a house with it. After that, real estate goes up 5% a year, on average. In 10 years, your house has appreciated 50% in value. (Don't worry about the math. I already did it for you.) That means it's worth $300,000, and you've made $100,000. Well ain't that just peachy.

But you could have taken your $200,000, borrowed another $300,000, and bought a house worth $500,000. (The math is still accurate. Whether or not the bank would lend you $300,000 is another story. Let's just pretend for a moment. You have a job that pays you $100,000 a year. You're married to the daughter of Mr. Velcro. You're a famous actor. I'm the King of Persia, remember?)

If houses appreciate at 5% a year, in 10 years your more expensive house would be worth $750,000. Now you've made $250,000. By borrowing money, you have $150,000 more than you'd have by paying strictly cash. And you have a much nicer house, too.

Who'd Lend Me the Money?

If you choose a good house, in a good location, a bank will lend you money. Banks like to lend money for property that holds its value. After all, if you can't meet your payments, the bank can take your house and sell it to get its money back.

Depending on your circumstances, all you need is 10% down. That means you'd need $10,000 for a $100,000 house. If you want to figure out how to accumulate $10,000, go back and read the chapter on saving. Or borrow the money from relatives, friends, former hockey coaches, etc.

Cabbages and Mortgages

A cabbage is a vegetable with leaves the size of baseball gloves.

A mortgage is what you have when you use your property as security for a loan. You can eat a cabbage. You can't eat a mortgage.

Until you pay back the loan, the person who holds the mortgage has a claim on your property.

High-ratio Man

There are two basic types of mortgage: conventional and high-ratio. The difference involves the amount of down payment required.

To obtain a conventional mortgage, you need to pay 25% or more of the value of your property as a down payment. The loan secured by the mortgage cannot exceed 75% of the property's appraised value.

If you put down less than 25%, you'll get a high-ratio mortgage. If you're buying a house, such a loan must be insured by the Canada

Mortgage Housing Corporation (CMHC) or the Mortgage Insurance Corporation of Canada (MICC).

There's a reason for all this. Say you borrow money to buy a house, and you put down 10% of its total appraised value to secure a loan to cover the rest of its value. A couple of months later, property values fall by 15%. (It happens.) At this point, your property is worth less than the total amount of your loan. If you stop paying the money back, the lender is stuck with a house that's not worth as much as he lent to you. That's why he won't lend to you unless you insure the loan.

Who's on First? What? No, He's on Second

You can obtain as many mortgages on your house as you want, as long as you can find someone who's willing to lend you money based on the remaining value of your property.

The first mortgage is the most secure. If you walk away from your loan, the holder of the first mortgage can seize your house, sell it, and take the value of his loan.

With a second mortgage, the lender takes the remaining value of your house after deducting the amount of your first mortgage and lends you money based on that amount. A second mortgage is often used to obtain a personal loan or a line of credit. If you default, the holder of the second mortgage gets paid only after the first mortgage holder. Because the lender in a second mortgage incurs a higher risk, he'll charge a higher rate of interest.

A third mortgage carries an even higher rate of interest and presents a correspondingly higher risk to the lender. If you need a third mortgage, you're usually living in the wrong house.

Looney Lingo

With an OPEN MORTGAGE, you can pay off the principal at any time without paying a penalty.

To pay off a CLOSED MORTGAGE, you often have to pay up to three months of interest to compensate the lender for his lost future revenues.

Many mortgages come with pre-payment clauses that allow you to pay back a specified amount — say, 10% — of the outstanding principal without paying a penalty.

If It Ain't Fixed, It's Variable

To repay most mortgages, you make monthly blended payments that include interest and principal. Initially, most of the total payment is interest.

With a fixed-rate mortgage, the monthly payment, and the proportion of interest to principal, remain constant for the life of the term.

With a variable-rate mortgage, the proportion of interest to principal fluctuates from month to month according to the prime rate. If the prime rate rises, so will the proportion of interest to principal in your mortgage payment. But the total monthly payment remains constant.

If you think interest rates will decline, go for the variable rate.

If rates are rising, or you prefer not to think about it, then you should lock in your mortgage at a fixed rate.

When the Moon Hits Your Eye Like a Big Pizza Pie, That's Amore. Then There's Amortization. That's Something Else Again

Amortization refers to the length of time over which you will repay your entire mortgage. The amortization period of a standard mortgage usually runs from 15 to 25 years. But you can amortize your mortgage over 10 years if you want, or over 30 years.

The longer the amortization, the more interest you pay over the life of the mortgage. The monthly payments on a 25-year mortgage are usually less than the monthly payments on a 10-year mortgage for an equivalent amount. But you'll make more payments over 25 years, and you'll end up paying a lot more in total.

However, many people can't afford the payments on a loan amortized over 10 years. So they take a loan amortized over 25 years, because they can afford the payments.

Amortization Made Even More Boring (But Read This If You Want to Save Loadsa Dough)

If you take 25 years to pay off your mortgage rather than 15, you'll end up paying an enormous amount more money. Take a typical $100,000 mortgage amortized over 25 years at 10%: It will cost you about $894 a month in payments. Multiply $894 by 12 months by 25 years, you get $268,200. For a $100,000 loan, you'll pay $268,200.

Now take that $100,000 loan and amortize it over 15 years. This will knock 10 years off the amount of time you have to repay your loan. But your monthly payments will increase by only about 16%, to $1,062. Now multiply $1,062 by 12 months by 15 years, and you'll get $191,160.

In other words, you'll save over $77,000 on your $100,000 mortgage.

As I said, some people can't afford to pay $1,000 a month, but they can afford to pay $894. But if you can afford it, shorten the amortization period.

Terms of Endearment (OK, I'm Scraping the Bottom of the Barrel. Somebody Has to Write These Stupid Titles)

The term describes the length of time over which the mortgage agreement remains in force. Your monthly payments remain constant over the term of the mortgage. If you have a fixed-rate mortgage, the rate of interest that you pay remains constant over the term as well.

You might choose a five-year term, for example, or even a seven-year or 10-year term. (In the good old days, banks used to sell mortgages with 25-year terms.) You can also get a mortgage with a six-month term.

When the mortgage comes up for renewal, then you select an appropriate term again.

The term of the mortgage has nothing to do with the amortization period.

What Kind of Term Am I?

If you think you know which way interest rates will move, choose your term accordingly. (And give me a call. I'd like to speak to you.)

If you think interest rates have hit their lowest point and will likely rise over the next five years, choose a five-year term. If you think they're going lower, choose a six-month term so you can renew your mortgage at a lower rate in six months.

If you just want to stop thinking about interest rates and start thinking about balloon racing in Chile, get a five-year term and put it out of your mind.

It's Not What You Want, It's What You Can Afford

As a general rule, lenders assume that you can afford to pay up to 30% of the gross family income each month in mortgage payments. If your annual family income is $50,000, then you can comfortably afford to pay about $1,250 a month in mortgage payments. If the family income is $40,000, then you can comfortably afford to pay $1,000 a month. (You can get pre-printed tables that will show you all this stuff from your bank.)

A Month Is a Matter of Weeks

If you don't qualify for a 15-year mortgage, you can get a 25-year mortgage and arrange to pay it back in weekly rather than monthly installments. Instead of making 12 monthly payments, you make 52 weekly payments, which actually works out to the equivalent of 13 months of payments. With an extra month a year, you can knock 10 years off your mortgage.

However, you should make sure that the lender calculates the interest on your loan no more frequently than once every six months. If the interest is calculated more frequently, you pay too much interest to make it worth your while to make weekly payments.

A Week by Any Other Name

Making weekly payments forces you to apply some discipline to paying off your mortgage quickly.

You can get the same result by making an additional yearly payment toward the principal. Almost all mortgage policies allow you to do this on the renewal date.

The Cost of an Affordable House

To calculate the maximum price that you can afford for a new house, multiply your family's gross annual income by three. If the gross family income is $50,000, then you can afford a house worth $150,000.

If you already own a house, you can add the equity in your house to this figure.

This calculation gives you a rough estimate.

Your lender may not agree, and probably won't. So use this calculation only as a rule of thumb.

More Interesting Stuff (Well, It's Sort of Interesting If You Like Dividing and Subtracting and Scratching Your Head a Lot)

You have to pay a penalty to refinance your mortgage before the renewal date. But if interest rates drop by 2% or more below your current rate, then you should consider refinancing, penalty or no penalty, especially if you still have a few years remaining on your term.

For example, say you have four years remaining on your $100,000 mortgage at 10%. Your banker says he'll charge you $4,000 in penalty fees to break it. But interest rates have fallen to 8% from 10%.

To see if the switch is worth the price, subtract the current interest rate from the rate you're paying (10% − 8% = 2%). Then multiply that by the number of years left in the term (2% x 4 years = 8%) and multiply the existing mortgage by that figure ($100,000 x 8% = $8,000) to get the total saving in interest.

DOLLARS AND SENSE

If you can't afford to pay the refinancing charge outright, just add it to the new mortgage. If your banker says he can't do that, take your business somewhere else.

In this case, even after paying a $4,000 penalty, you still save $4,000 in interest. So it makes sense to make the switch.

Things to Remember at Renewal Time

➤ A mortgage is the cheapest loan you can get, so when the time comes to renew it, consider incorporating an additional amount to use for purposes other than paying for your house. Do you want to

remodel your kitchen? take a cruise around the Pacific? send little Billy-Bob to summer camp for three months? Now's the time to do it.

➤ Renewal time is also a good time to pay down your mortgage. Even a little extra can go a long way toward paying the mortgage off more quickly.

➤ If interest rates fall when the time comes to re-finance, don't change your monthly payments. That way, more of your money will go towards the principal, and you'll pay off the mortgage more quickly.

Don't Pay Cash, Even If You Have It (Give It to Me Instead. I'll Meet You Anywhere. Just Give Me a Call. Put the Cash in a Bag. Leave It on My Porch. Honest. I Don't Mind)

If you have $100,000, don't use it to buy a $100,000 house. Instead, use it as a down payment on a $500,000 house.

If housing prices double in 20 years, a $100,000 house will be worth $200,000. But a $500,000 house will be worth $1 million.

In general, the bigger the mortgage, the better the investment. You should buy the biggest house you can get. It's the only thing we own that goes up in value tax free. (We've talked about this before. It's worth repeating. I have to say the same thing twice anyway to get you to pay attention to me. Is it my hair you don't like or what?)

Other Nit-picks Regarding Mortgages

➤ Interest Adjustment Date: If the mortgage lender advances funds before the first or the last day of the month, he can't charge you a full month of interest. So he'll calculate the interest owing until the first day of the following month, and take the appropriate amount at that time.

➤ Property Taxes: If you have a high-ratio mortgage, the financial in-stitution will insist that it pay your property taxes. (This is to ensure that you don't fall into arrears on your taxes. If you do, the city can seize your house. Obviously, the bank doesn't want this to happen. It wants to seize your house instead.)

You make mortgage payments every month, but taxes fall due twice a year. So you should try to get the bank to pay interest on the money it holds to pay your taxes. The interest could easily amount to $100 to $150 a year.

Ideally, you should pay your own property taxes.

Approval-seeking

If you're looking for a house, and you think today's interest rate is as good as it will get, you can apply to your financial institution for a pre-approved mortgage. You'll receive a pre-authorized mortgage at a rate guaranteed for 90 days. If you find a house within that period, you won't have to pay more for a mortgage if interest rates go up. A pre-approval will impress the seller of a house, because it provides reassurance that you can pay for the property.

Naturally, the bank will still appraise the house and make sure it meets any other specifications before you can turn the pre-approval into cash. So your offer should be conditional upon financing.

Vendor, Take That Back, You Mutha

To sell a house more quickly, the seller will sometimes agree to provide the buyer with a loan for some of the purchase price, usually at a better rate of interest than the buyer could get at a bank.

The buyer then makes regular mortgage payments to the seller. The seller is also called the vendor. (Sometimes the seller is called a lot of other things, but we won't go into that here.) That's why this arrangement is called a vendor take-back.

Banks, Trust Companies, or Mortgage Brokers: Where's the Beef?

If the property that you want does not already carry a low-interest mortgage that you can assume, and if the vendor will not take back a mortgage, then you have to get financing from another source. Most people first try a bank. But banks apply very strict standards to a client's income, credit rating, and other qualifications. Banks also tend to make decisions slowly.

Trust companies are usually much more aggressive and will often provide a better deal than a bank. But they're also quite strict when it comes to income and credit rating.

Mortgage brokers can usually offer the lowest rates possible, because they often deal with smaller trust companies, foreign bank subsidiaries and finance companies. Even a saving of $1/4\%$ to $1/2\%$ can add up to thousands of dollars over the life of a mortgage.

On the other hand, if you don't qualify for a mortgage from a conventional source, a mortgage broker can often provide you with a mortgage, but will charge you a higher rate to compensate for the increased risk.

You can find a good mortgage broker through your lawyer, accountant, or real estate representative, or just look in the Yellow Pages. Always talk to more than one and compare their fees.

Mortgage vs. RRSP: Battle of Boredom (Warning: More Math Ahead)

Let's assume that you have an extra $5,000, and you're not sure whether to use it to pay down your mortgage or invest in an RRSP (or buy 6,000 cartons of potato chips so you won't run out over the next 25 years while you sit in your house and pay for it).

If you use the $5,000 to pay down your mortgage at 10%, then you'll save about $500 in interest. However, if you invest the $5,000 in an RRSP, you'll do better. Here's why.

First, you get a tax deduction. If you make between $30,000 and $60,000 a year, the deduction is worth 42% of your total contribution. On $5,000, that's a $2,100 tax rebate.

Now you can take that $2,100 and use it to pay down your mortgage. It's a win, win, strategy.

Here's an Easy Way

If you ever want to know whether you should pay down your mortgage or invest in your RRSP, just take a blank piece of paper. On one side, write your mortgage interest rate. On the other side, write your marginal tax rate. For most of us it's 42%. If your marginal tax rate is higher, then put the money into your RRSP. If your mortgage interest is higher, then you're dealing with a loan shark and you shouldn't meet him in a dark alley.

Can I Make My Mortgage Tax Deductible?

When you borrow to make an investment in a mutual fund, for example, you can deduct the interest on the loan from your total taxed income.

When you borrow to buy a house, you can't deduct the interest payments from your total taxable income.

So if you have any investments (outside your RRSP), you should cash them in, use the proceeds to pay down your mortgage, then borrow the same amount to repurchase your investments. Now you can deduct the interest on your loan from your taxable income.

You still own $50,000 worth of investments, and you still owe the bank $50,000, but now the interest on that $50,000 is completely tax deductible.

Even if you have $5,000 in investments, you can still get the same advantage. Cash in those CSBs and GICs, pay your $50,000 mortgage down to $45,000, and then take out a personal loan for $5,000 to invest. That way, $1/10$th ($5,000) of your mortgage becomes tax deductible.

Inspector, There's a Fly in My Soup

Most people buy a house because they like the colour of the wallpaper, the layout of the second-floor bedrooms, the way the kitchen doors lead into a sunporch, the colour of the hardwood floors — all sorts of reasons that have nothing to do with the quality of the house.

In fact, your dream house may be a house of horrors.

An inspector can alert you to potential horror stories. Will those beams last another five years? Will that chimney fall down in a heavy wind? Will the insulation help you to keep the house warm without burning half of Canada's oil and gas output? Is that daylight coming through the roof over there?

For a fee of $200 to $300, an inspector may save you from a decision you'll regret.

Location, Location, Location

As any real estate agent will tell you, there are three criteria to consider in choosing a house: location, location, and location. (Having said that, you might also consider location. Drums. Cymbals. Loud groans.)

People lose money on real estate more often because the location is bad than because the house itself doesn't measure up. You can always fix a house. You can't do much about the eight-lane street that passes in front of it.

Some Questions to Ask Yourself

➤ Are there schools nearby?

➤ Are there sidewalks?

➤ Parks?

➤ Public transit?

➤ Is the neighbourhood well-established?

➤ Is it safe?

➤ Are there any children around to play with my little Frodo?

➤ Is the area quiet, or is that a crack house next door?

The Best Time to Buy a House

The best time to buy a house is in the winter. Here's why.

Like the price of everything else, the price of real estate depends on supply and demand. House prices rise when you have more buyers than sellers. When you have more sellers than buyers, they fall.

Most people look for a house in the summer. They don't look for a house in the winter unless they have to. It's cold. It gets dark early. The kids have to wear galoshes and snowsuits and mittens and hats or stay at home with Heavy Barbara, the babysitter.

So now's your chance. If you're the only one who's willing to trudge through the snow to look at yet another two-bedroom handy-man's special, you could get yourself a good deal.

Agents: The Scoop

Real estate agents get paid by the seller of the property, not the buyer. They deduct their commission from the total selling price before the seller gets a penny.

With this in mind, real estate agents look for good properties to sell. The more properties they can sell, the more money they make.

Having said that, a good real estate agent can help you buy a house. But you shouldn't expect the agent to do the work for you. Only you know what you want in a house. And real estate agents don't read minds. (They don't do windows, either.)

In fact, a good real estate agent will get you started, point you in the right direction, give you a few suggestions of properties in your price range, then send you on your way. Any real estate agent who drives you hither and yon, day in, day out, for weeks on end while you waffle and dither and make up your mind — any real estate agent who does that has too much time on his hands and probably doesn't know what he's doing.

When you finally decide to buy a house, a real estate agent will begin to earn her fee. And she'll do much more than just negotiate a good price. She'll advise you on financing; devise innovative terms that fit your circumstances and accommodate the seller; and help you through the inevitable tensions that arise when you're dealing with a purchase worth $100,000 or more. (How many times do you lay out that kind of dough for anything?)

Selling a House

An agent can advise you on setting a price for your house. First, the agent will analyze your needs. Do you need money fast? Have you already bought another house? Can you afford to wait until you get your asking price? Then the agent will place your house and its characteristics in the context of the neighbourhood. How much have

Facts for a Buck

If you go to an open house, the agent who greets you at the door automatically becomes your representative unless your own agent accompanies you. That means the agent ends up negotiating for the buyer and the seller. It's not an ideal situation.

similar houses sold for? How long did it take to sell them? (And by the way, who's the guy with the funny hat who just moved into 106?)

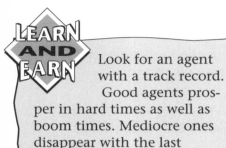

Look for an agent with a track record. Good agents prosper in hard times as well as boom times. Mediocre ones disappear with the last inflated sale.

Questions, the Sequel

Here are some questions to ask a real estate agent:

➤ How long have you been a real estate agent?

➤ Do you live in the area?

➤ How many houses have you sold in your career?

➤ What kind of service will you give me?

Don't Forget to Negotiate

Every dollar you save can be used to make another investment. So whether you're buying or selling, always negotiate.

Questions, Part 78

➤ Why are you selling?

➤ Is the asking price firm or flexible?

➤ If someone bought your house today, how much would you take for it?

The Six Key Words to Negotiating Success

You can do better than that.

The Seller's Golden Rule

Never let the buyer know your bottom price.

Now for the Lawyers

Your agent will help you complete an agreement of purchase and sale. Your banker will help you with the financing. Now, like it or not, you need a lawyer.

Choose one who specializes in real estate. The lawyer will make sure that the seller actually owns the property. (You'd be amazed....) The lawyer will also find out if the owner owes any money to contractors for that nice new kitchen that he never paid for. If he does, the contractor can block the sale until he gets his money. The lawyer will also check to see that the realty taxes have been paid and review any other legal aspects involved.

Insurance: Better to Be Safe Than Sorry

It's better to have insurance and not need it than to need insurance and not have it.

Besides, most mortgage lenders demand that you buy homeowners' insurance. After all, they own most of the house. You just pay for it.

Tips for Insuring

➤ You should insure your home for at least 80% of its replacement value.

➤ Over time, your house will rise in value. Your insurance coverage should rise along with it.

➤ Insure the contents of your home for their replacement value, not for the original price that you paid for them.

➤ If you run a business out of your home, make sure that your homeowners' policy covers it.

You've Bought One. How About Another?

As long as you understand the potential risks and rewards of owning real estate, then go ahead: Buy another house. You can rent it to cover your costs and make some money on your investment.

A rental property can provide you with an income while appreciating in value. If you sell it, you'll have to pay taxes on the increase in value. But in the meantime, you gain a lot of tax advantages from owning property. You can write off your expenses, for example, including the interest on your mortgage.

Not for the Faint of Heart

Owning property sounds easy. You just sit back and watch the rent pour in. But if you take that approach, the roof soon starts to leak, the walls crumble, the furnace stops working, birds build their nests in the attic, and no one will live in the place.

It takes work to maintain a rental property. You have to watch over it, nurture it, just as you would if you lived there.

You have to find good tenants, who pay their rent on time. (When they do, you have to keep a record of the payment.) And when they call you at two in the morning because the hot water pipe has sprung a leak inside the wall, you have to respond.

Unless you hire a property management company to do all this for you, at a fee, you should live close enough to the property to keep an eye on it.

How Real Is This Estate?

There are two types of real estate: raw land and developed land.

Raw land is just that: no buildings, no sidewalks, no sewers, roads, hydro, or shopping centres. It's just vacant undeveloped land.

Sewers, roads, hydro facilities, streetlights, and sidewalks all cost money and require permits and licences to install. They also add value to property. The more developed the property, the higher the purchase price.

If I Buy Two Do I Get a Discount?

The price of real estate is determined by the property's productive capacity. The more money the property can generate, the more value it has.

If you buy raw land, you can use it for family picnics or flying a kite. Otherwise, it will just sit there until you find a buyer. Meanwhile, you have to pay taxes from your own pocket, because the land is generating no income.

If you buy a farm, however, then you can rent the land to a farmer.

If you buy a parking lot, you can rent spaces to people who want to park their cars. In the meantime, the property may or may not appreciate in value.

If a property is not operating at its highest productive capacity, then you can usually purchase it at a discount, increase its productive capacity, and sell it for substantially more money.

Facts for a Buck

Undeveloped land that does not produce an income has little value as collateral on a loan. So you can't borrow as much to cover the cost of the property.

If It Sounds Too Good to Be True, It Usually Is, and Other Tales of Woe

Lots of real estate companies would like to sell you a house or a condo in Florida, Arizona, or the Caribbean. They have pretty pictures to show you. And good stories about the beach, the weather, the cheap food, the friendly people, and yaddy, yaddy, blabbety, blah.

Tell them to join Uncle Sylvester in the sandbox.

You should never buy real estate from a picture in a magazine or video. The video won't show the landfill site next door, and the photo won't convey the odour of the rendering plant in the backyard.

Location, Location, and Location

Make sure your home is in a well-established area. When it comes to real estate, you don't want to be a jack of all trades, and master of none. You want professional help.

Read It and Reap

➤ Your home is one of the biggest investments that you'll ever make. Be sure you're financially and emotionally ready to make the move.

➤ Can you afford to tie up your initial investment for a long time?

➤ Is your credit rating good?

➤ Do you have the time and talent to effectively supervise your property?

➤ A house is a long-term investment. Over the long term, real estate prices have gone up. Over the short to intermediate term, prices can remain stable or fall.

➤ Don't forget about saving through your RRSP and other vehicles. Real estate is only one part of a solid financial equation.

➤ The bigger the house, the better the investment. But don't buy more house than you can comfortably afford.

➤ As a rule of thumb, you should not spend more than 30% of your gross family income on mortgage payments, property taxes, and energy bills.

➤ You can get hurt badly by speculating with the family home. Many people made money flipping properties in the real estate boom of the 1980s. But many more lost it all when the market peaked.

➤ The three most important considerations when buying real estate are location, location, and location.

➤ In buying a house, your team should include a real estate agent, lawyer, and banker.

➤ To repay most mortgages, you make monthly blended payments that include interest and principal. Initially, most of the total payment is interest.

➤ To calculate the maximum price that you can afford for a new house, multiply your family's gross annual income by three.

➤ If you have $100,000, don't use it to buy a $100,000 house. Instead, use it as a down payment on a $500,000 house.

➤ It usually works to your benefit to invest any extra money in an RRSP, then use the tax rebate to pay down your mortgage.

➤ If you have any investments (outside your RRSP), you should cash them in, use the proceeds to pay down your mortgage, then borrow the same amount to repurchase your investments. Now you can deduct the interest on your loan from your taxable income.

➤ Never buy a property without first having it inspected by a professional.

➤ The best time to buy a house is in the winter.

➤ Always try to negotiate to get a better deal.

➤ If you want something, ask for it. The worst that can happen is the seller will say no.

Chapter 9

RRSPs: Too Soon Old, Too Late Smart

> **In This Chapter**
> ➤ What's an RRSP?
> ➤ Do I need one?
> ➤ How much can I contribute?
> ➤ Self-directed RRSPs. Spousal RRSPs.
> ➤ RRIFs. Annuities. RESPs.

First In, Last Out

For most Canadians, RRSPs are the first investment they'll ever make and the last investment they'll ever need.

Most kids think they're too young to think about retirement. That's a big mistake. If you're fortunate enough, start one of these things when you're young, you'll never have to worry when you're old.

Unfortunately, most of us spend our time and money when we're young on everything but an RRSP. And even our parents don't tell us not to. Too bad.

If RRSPs were devised by anybody but the government, they might be more popular. Because they're associated with the government, some people think they're just another trick devised to separate us from our hard-earned money.

Who's Driving?

Even people who have RRSPs don't really know how they work. They don't realize, for example, that they can move their

> **Facts for a Buck**
>
> RRSP stands for Registered Retirement Savings Plan, but don't let the word retirement scare you. This plan is for everyone, even you.

money, within an RRSP, into all sorts of investments, from guaranteed investment certificates to mutual funds to stocks and bonds. Often they just give their money to the bank and say, "This is for my RRSP." That's like handing a cab driver a $100 bill and saying, "Take me for a ride."

It's What's Inside That Counts

Think of an RRSP as a briefcase. The briefcase keeps its contents protected from elements outside. In the case of an RRSP, the briefcase protects your money from the sticky-fingered tentacles of the government. On money held in an RRSP, you pay no taxes. And when you first put the money into an RRSP, you can deduct it from your total annual income when you're calculating your income tax for the year.

That means you pay less tax. And your money grows tax-free.

Keep Your Eye On It

Once the money's in an RRSP, you shouldn't just forget about it. It's like any other investment. It can grow quickly, it can grow slowly, sometimes it grows not at all, and sometimes it even loses value. The big difference between money invested in an RRSP and money invested in Uncle Hughie's Bean Farm is that your RRSP investment grows tax-free.

Outside an RRSP, your money may earn $100, and you'd pay, say, $25 in tax, leaving you with $75. Inside an RRSP, your money may make $100, and you'd pay no tax. So you still have $100 left to re-invest.

The Same Lesson, Over and Over Again

If you were paying attention, airhead, you'll remember our chapter on saving and the passages on compound interest. Over a few years, you'll accumulate a lot more money with $100 reinvested over and over than you will with $75. (If I have to tell you this one more time, I'll set your underwear on fire.)

Here's Another Way to Say the Same Thing, Again, Already

There are two reasons why everyone under the age of 69 should own an RRSP. (If you're over 69, why aren't you out lawn bowling?)

First: You'll save taxes.

Second: You'll save taxes.

If you earn $40,000 this year and don't invest a penny in an RRSP (gadzooks, you ninny!) you'll pay tax on the entire $40,000.

However, if you invest $5,000 of that $40,000 into an RRSP, then Revenue Canada will tax only the remaining $35,000 of your $40,000 salary.

If you invest that $5,000 in a good mutual fund, you should be able to earn 15% to 18% a year, on average. At 15% a year, that $5,000 will become $20,250 in just 10 years. That's 20 big ones, with enough left over for 25 medium pizzas.

Stuff You Don't Really Care About Anyway

You may earn $40,000 from your job. But you may also run a business or own rental property that makes money. Lucky you. The money you make is added to your earned income. So is alimony, if you're collecting it (at least at the time of writing this book).

If you pay alimony, or own a business or a rental property that loses money, you deduct the losses from the income you get from your job to calculate your total earned income.

What to Do on Your Summer Vacation

All these details and more are available in all those boring little booklets that Revenue Canada distributes with your income tax form. For a really good time, try reading one of those books from cover to cover. For an even better time, try reading two.

The Sky — or 18% — Is the Limit

You can contribute up to 18% of your earned income from the previous year, to a maximum of $13,500. This limit is frozen until the year 2003. Then it rises to $14,500 in 2004 and to $15,500 in 2005. In the following year, the limit will be indexed. (This could all change again in future years, if the government decides it needs the money.) For those of us who may still have time to contribute to our RRSPs before 2006, this comes as good news. For the rest of us — well, now we know how Rocket Richard felt when hockey players' salaries went up. (Okay, he probably felt worse. But you get the idea.)

The contribution limit applies to all our contributions to a registered pension fund, whether we make them ourselves or they're made on our behalf (with our money, don't forget) by our employer. Most of us work full time for an employer, who deposits a portion of our earnings into a company pension plan. That means we have to subtract our pension contributions (PA) from our total maximum RRSP contribution — 18% of last year's earned income — to determine the amount that we can contribute ourselves.

A Calculation

If you earned $40,000 in 1997 and paid $1,500 into your company's pension plan, you could contribute up to $5,700 into your 1997 RRSP. Here's the calculation:

1. Multiply $40,000 by 18% to determine your maximum contribution;

2. Subtract the $1,500 that you paid into your company plan;

3. If you came up with $5,700, give yourself a kiss.

Kiss Your Employer, Too

Fortunately, your employer will do most of this number-crunching for you. You'll find your annual pension contribution (called a pension adjustment) on your T4 slip each year.

And you don't have to do the rest of this calculation to find your maximum RRSP contribution limit, because Revenue Canada does it for you and sends you a computerized statement each year that shows your contribution limit.

Tax, or a Lesson in How Society Works

Your marginal tax rate determines the amount of tax that you'll save by investing in an RRSP. For most of us, our marginal tax rate is the amount of tax we pay on every dollar we earn in annual salary. The more we earn, the more we pay. (Makes you wonder why anyone bothers to work harder, doesn't it?)

Another Calculation That Will Make You Cry

These were the marginal tax rates for the average Canadian last year. (They vary a bit depending on the province where you live):

Taxable income	Marginal rate
Up to $29,590	27%
$29,590 to $59,180	42%
Above $59,180	52%

The Calculation in Action (Block That Kick!)

If you earn $40,000 a year, your marginal tax rate will be about 42%. So if you contribute $5,000 to an RRSP, you will save yourself $2,100 in taxes. (Multiply $5,000 x 42%.)

If you hadn't invested $5,000 in an RRSP, you'd pay that tax — $2,100 — to the government.

For someone earning $65,000 a year, who pays 52% of his earned income in taxes, a $5,000 contribution would save $2,600. (Multiply $5,000 by 52%. That comes to $2,600. Whew!)

If this fellow hadn't invested $5,000 in an RRSP, he'd pay $2,600 to the government.

Doesn't it make more sense to put the money into an RRSP?

More Boring Details About RRSPs

You don't have to take your tax deduction in the same year as you make your contribution. You can claim it in any future year.

Believe it or not, this can come in handy. If your income goes up in a couple of years, you'll pay tax at a higher rate. The more you make, the more the government takes.

If you're taxed at a higher rate, then your contribution is worth more in terms of the money you'll save in taxes.

On the other hand, unless your taxable income now falls within the lowest federal tax bracket, and your salary increase would raise it to the middle or top tax bracket, you might as well take your refund now.

Inside RRSPs: The True Story

On money held within an RRSP, the interest, dividends, and capital gains can grow at a compound rate, tax-free. You don't pay tax on the money until you withdraw it from the plan. Ideally, you won't do that until you're really old and wheezing around the lawn-bowling arena in a little buggy with your lunch in a thermos.

Because they have to pay tax on the money when they remove it from an RRSP, many people wonder why they should bother investing in an RRSP at all.

Here's why: Even after you pay the tax when you remove your money from an RRSP, you still end up with substantially more than you'd have if you'd invested it outside an RRSP.

An Example (Warning: More Boring Math Ahead. In Cases of Severe Fatigue, Skip to the Last Sentence of This Section)

Ms. A invests $5,000 inside an RRSP.

Mr. B invests $5,000 outside an RRSP.

Each pays tax at a rate of 52% and earns 12% a year on the invested money.

Who has more 20 years down the road?

Ms. A has more than $70,000.

Mr. B has less than $34,000.

Mr. B continues to wear the same short-sleeved drip-dry white shirt as he's worn for 11 years to work in the ticket booth at the local bus terminal, while Ms. A retires to Honolulu with Brad, the young gardener.

(If you skipped that calculation, put one hand under your arm and sing "Have you seen your mother, baby, standing in the shadows?")

Why Did This Happen, Mike?

Why did this happen, you ask me? I'll tell you. The money invested in the RRSP earned interest on top of interest. Outside an RRSP, money earns interest, and then you pay tax on the interest, which cuts your earnings in half.

From Soup to Nuts (If You Like to Read the Labels on Your Cereal Boxes, You'll Love This)

You can keep almost any type of investment in your RRSP, from the soup of equities to the nuts of bonds. In general, the following investments qualify:

➤ Guaranteed investment certificates (GICs) and term deposits

➤ Money deposited in Canadian funds in a bank, trust company, or credit union

➤ Mutual funds registered with Revenue Canada

➤ Certain bonds (including Canada Savings Bonds), debentures, and similar obligations guaranteed by the Government of Canada, a province, a municipality, or a Crown corporation

➤ Shares, rights, warrants, and call options listed on stock exchanges in Montreal, Toronto, Winnipeg, Alberta, or Vancouver

➤ Shares of unlisted Canadian public corporations

➤ Shares listed on prescribed foreign stock exchanges, including Paris, London, New York, American, Mexican, National, Pacific Coast, Boston, Philadelphia-Baltimore, Chicago Board of Trade, Washington, Cincinnati, Pittsburgh, Detroit, Salt Lake, Mid West, Spokane, The American Exchange, and the NASDAQ (National Association of Securities Dealers Automated Quotation system)

➤ A bond, debenture, note, or similar obligation issued by a public corporation

➤ A mortgage secured by real property located in Canada, as long as certain conditions are met

➤ Mortgage-backed securities

➤ Qualifying retirement annuities

➤ Shares of small business corporations, subject to stringent requirements

➤ Contains no MSG or riboflavin

With All These Choices, What Are You Doing Here?

Most people put all their RRSP money in a savings account or GIC. That's dumb.

Would you put your children in the fruit cellar when they could be outside in the sunshine growing strong and healthy? Well, how do you expect your RRSP investments to grow if you let them languish in the financial equivalent of a dark hole?

Big Mike says, "Transfer those investments, now!"

Book Value

The book value of your RRSP is simply the amount of money that you've contributed to the plan.

Market Value

The market value of your RRSP is the amount that all your RRSP investments would fetch if you sold them all today.

If you contribute $1,000 to your RRSP, buying 100 shares of a mutual fund trading at $10 per share, your RRSP's book value will be $1,000.

If the share price rises to $15, your RRSP's market value will increase to $1,500. But its book value remains at $1,000.

As you'll see, there's a reason for explaining this distinction.

Sprächen Sie Français, etc.

As of 1994, you could invest up to 20% of your RRSP's book value outside of Canada. (That's why we bothered to explain the difference between book value and market value. You're welcome.)

The money you invest in your RRSP outside of Canada is called its foreign content. (Some people think Canadians should invest their RRSP money only in Canada. Other people say that money knows no boundaries, and we should be able to pursue opportunities no matter where they occur. If you want to argue about this, buy a suit and join the government.)

Foreign content includes mutual funds that invest primarily outside of Canada or individual stocks of companies that have incorporated outside of Canada.

Almost all shares traded on the New York, American, or NASDAQ Stock Exchanges are considered to be foreign content.

Back to the Book

If a foreign mutual fund rises substantially in value, it won't throw your RRSP's foreign-content ratio out of whack. (Book value is the amount you invest, remember? Pay attention, Lloyd, and take that pencil out of your ear.)

However, dividends from stocks in your RRSP that are automatically re-invested can add to the RRSP's book value. If your RRSP's foreign content exceeds the limit, the government will charge you 1% a month of the excess.

The financial institution that holds your RRSP will calculate the percentage of foreign exposure and let you know if you exceed the limit.

Mike's World

We should all try to maximize the foreign content in our RRSPs. Here's why: All the money that's invested in Canada adds up to only 3% of all the money in the world. That means 97% of the action goes on somewhere else.

Currency rates are another reason to invest outside Canada. In 1991, the Canadian dollar was worth US89¢. Three years later, it was worth US72¢. If you held a U.S. investment, and all it did was break even, you would have made money, because your U.S. dollars would be worth more than they were when you made the investment. (If you think I'm going to discuss the complexities of foreign exchange, you're crazy.)

Maximum Mike

If you don't make your maximum contribution this year, you can add the remaining eligible amount to your contribution next year, or the year after that, for up to seven years.

For example, say your 1993 maximum RRSP contribution was $5,700 and you contributed only $3,700. You're still eligible to contribute $2,000, and you can make this contribution any time over the next seven years, in addition to your maximum annual contribution for the year.

Don't Procrastinate, Donna

As your piano teacher says, don't put off till tomorrow what you can do today. You should always try to make your maximum contribution each year. First, the money in your RRSP starts to grow as soon as you invest it. If you wait to invest, your money won't grow.

Second, being the undisciplined pea-brain — no, wait, I didn't really mean that — being only human, you'll probably be tempted to spend the money elsewhere, if you ever get it. And then you'll never make the remaining RRSP contribution at all.

Over the Top

You're allowed to over-contribute to an RRSP to a maximum of $8,000 over the course of your lifetime. If you over-contribute by more than

$8,000, the government will charge you a penalty of 1% per month on the over-contribution. So if you have an extra $8,000 lying around, burning a hole through your sock drawer, you might want to over-contribute on purpose.

You won't be able to deduct it from your total taxable income. But it will earn interest, tax-free, inside the plan.

Another Calculation That You Might Want to Skip

If you can earn 15% on your money, you'll make about $1,200 each year on your additional $8,000 contribution.

If you made the over-contribution in January 1994, Revenue Canada won't tell you to remove it until you file your tax return the following year. Then you still have the rest of the year plus another full calendar year to remove the $8,000. You've already paid tax on it, so you don't have to pay tax on it again when you remove it.

In the meantime, the money earned on your $8,000 over-contribution during those three years of tax free compounding stays inside the plan. If you earned 15% a year, you've accumulated about $3,500.

If you can double that $3,500 every four years, you'll have $28,000 in 12 years. In 20 years you'll have $112,000. And in 32 years, you'll have $996,000. All for making an $8,000 mistake.

In fact, you don't have to remove the $8,000 at all. Instead, when the time comes, you can just use it as your RRSP contribution for that year.

Which Way to the RRSP Store?

You can set up an RRSP at any bank or trust company or through a financial planner, stockbroker, or life insurance agent.

It's easy. You fill out a form and sign it. A few weeks later, you get an official tax receipt in the mail.

How Many RRSPs Do I Need?

Some people buy an RRSP here and an RRSP there. Pretty soon they have an RRSP for every day of the week.

All you really need is one: a self-directed RRSP.

The Do-it-yourself RRSP

With a self-directed RRSP, you can include different investments within the same plan. Do you want a Canada Trust GIC? That's fine. Do you want a Royal Bank term deposit? That's fine, too. How about stocks, bonds, mutual funds, mortgage-backed securities, strip coupon bonds, or Canada Savings Bonds? Fine. They're all fine. Just fine. Fine, fine, fine and dandy. Bring 'em all home for dinner. That's bloody fine, too. Fine.

Get to the Point, Mike

The point is, you can hold all your RRSP investments within the same self-directed plan. This gives you the flexibility to change your investment mix at any time.

If one financial institution offers a better deal than the others, you can switch. And you no longer have to worry about deposit insurance, because you can put $60,000 in CIBC GICs, $60,000 in TD Bank term deposits. (Strip coupon bonds, mortgage-backed securities and Treasury bills have no limit.)

More Tax Talk

Most financial institutions handle self-administered RRSPs and charge an administration fee of about $100 to $150 for the service. You can deduct these administration fees from your taxable income. However, you can't deduct brokerage fees charged for the purchase or sale of securities within an RRSP.

The flexibility you get from a self-directed RRSP is worth the fee.

Oy, Mate, Make Mine a Double

If you're legally married, you can contribute a portion or all of your allowable contribution to your spouse's RRSP. Why would you do such a thing? Taxes, what else?

If your spouse earns less than you do and pays tax at a lower rate, then you both save on income tax. First, you claim the tax deduction, even though you contribute to your spouse's RRSP.

Then, when your spouse withdraws the money from the spousal plan, your spouse reports the income and pays the taxes, presumably at a lower rate.

You have to leave the money in the plan for two years or more. Otherwise, the contributing spouse gets taxed.

Name That Spouse

Do people really live with a spouse? It sounds like some kind of little round fur-covered rubber dingus that you'd keep in a tool chest. "Honey, bring up the spouse, will you, and don't forget the plunger."

If you can think up a better word for spouse, we'll send you 100 copies of Revenue Canada's latest *Income Tax Handbook*. Second prize: 200 copies.

A No-dough Spouse

If your spouse doesn't work, throw the bum out.

Otherwise, if your feeling generous, and your spouse has no earned income, you can still contribute on your spouse's behalf to an RRSP. It doesn't matter if your spouse has any earned income or not. Nor does it matter if your spouse has already made the maximum contribution to an RRSP. What matters is your own contribution. And the fact that you live with a hairy little spouse at all.

There Are Limits, You Know

Your combined contribution to your own and your spouse's RRSP cannot exceed your personal contribution limit. And to get really ridiculous, you can contribute to your spouse's RRSP even if you're over age 69, providing you still have earned income and your spouse is not over the age of 69.

I'll bet you're really glad to know that.

Home, Sweet Home

Introduced in the 1992 federal budget, the Home Buyers' Plan allows individuals to withdraw funds tax free from their RRSPs and use the money to purchase a home from someone else.

Then they have to pay the money back to their RRSP.

The home can take the form of a house, mobile home, apartment, condominium, or co-operative. (That refrigerator carton isn't a home. Sorry, Bluto.)

You can withdraw up to $20,000 tax-free. That means a couple can withdraw up to $40,000. (What about a triple? Who let you into this book?)

Here's the catch: You have to pay the money back over 15 equal annual installments. These payments are not tax-deductible. If you miss a payment or make only a partial payment, then your taxable income will be increased by the amount of the shortfall.

Beware: More Math Ahead

If you borrow $15,000 from your RRSP, then you'll have to repay it in annual installments of $1,000 apiece over the next 15 years.

If you pay only $600 one year, you'll have to pay tax on the remaining $400 of the annual installment.

The first installment must be made by the end of the second year following the year of the withdrawal. If you removed the money in 1994, the first installment payment would not be due until the end of 1996.

The Fine Print

Before you can remove the money from your RRSP, you must have a written agreement to acquire a qualifying home that will be used as your primary residence within one year of purchase. The home must be located in Canada, and it must be your main year-round residence.

It doesn't matter whether the home is new, used, or under construction. Nor does it matter whether this is the first home you've ever bought. However, you cannot use the plan to pay for a home that you've already purchased.

Participants in the plan can make RRSP contributions in the same year in which they make the withdrawal. But you have to make the contribution at least 91 days before you withdraw the money.

Some Good Points and Bad Points

Good point: The Home Buyers' Plan enables young people to make a down payment on a home they couldn't otherwise afford.

Bad point: Since you've removed the money from your RRSP, your tax-sheltered retirement fund can no longer grow at a compound rate. (Here comes some more math.) Once you remove the money, it's a lot harder than you think to catch up.

For example, at age 31, you withdraw $10,000 from your RRSP and use it as a down payment on a house. Then you pay back the money in 15 annual installments. At age 69, you'll have about $85,000 in your RRSP, assuming a 7% annual return.

If you'd left the money in your RRSP to compound tax-free, assuming that same 7% yield, you'd have about $150,000 in the plan at age 69.

(On the other hand, your house might increase in value too. But that's not a sure thing. Compound growth within an RRSP is.)

Who Goes There?

The best investments to hold inside your RRSP are mutual funds. In fact, whether you hold them inside or outside your RRSP, mutual funds should make up the majority of your portfolio.

Investment advisors used to recommend keeping interest-bearing investments inside your RRSP and investments that accumulate dividends and capital gains outside your RRSP. That's because you pay tax on unprotected interest income; you don't pay tax on your first $100,000 in capital gains.

But today, with interest rates so low, that doesn't make sense. Instead, your goal should be: maximum yield through long-term growth.

You can obtain maximum yield through long-term growth from a diversified portfolio of mutual funds.

Sylvia and Willy

Compare two investors:

➤ Sylvia the Snake Charmer invests $2,000 a year in an RRSP composed of GICs earning 6% annually.

➤ Slick Willy makes the same $2,000 RRSP contribution, except that his RRSP is composed of good quality equity mutual funds earning 16% a year.

Poor Sylvia. In 30 years, she'll have $167,603. Slick Willy will have more than $1.2 million. Who's better off? (Anybody want to buy a snake?)

Return of Sylvia and Willy

You don't have to keep all your money in mutual funds. But you should invest at least some of it there. Even if they return just 1% more than your other investments, they can still make a huge difference down the road.

For example, Sylvia the Snake Charmer makes a $2,000 annual contribution to her RRSP and earns 13% on her money. In 30 years she'll have $662,630.

Slick Willy's investments earn just 1% more. At 14%, he has $813,474 after 30 years.

That extra 1% yield was worth an additional $150,844.

A Pinch of This, a Cup of That...

A solid conservative RRSP portfolio might consist of Canadian and foreign equity funds, income and bond funds, some GICs, CSBs, money market funds, and gold.

➤ The equity fund provides the maximum long-term growth.

➤ The income and bond funds provide the steady stream of income, year after year.

➤ The cash component of the portfolio is the slush fund, providing both safety and available capital to scoop up bargains as prices fall in other areas.

➤ The gold fund provides potential for growth while maintaining purchasing power.

Invest Now, Profit Later

Many people follow a ritual when they make their annual RRSP contribution. They stand outside a trust company in the freezing cold, stamping their feet and blowing on their fingers, talking to the same people they met last year at the same time, in the same place.

You have to stop meeting this way.

First of all, you're making your contribution at the very last minute, at the end of the year. (At least, I hope you are. If you're standing around in the snow when you don't have to, you need more than this book.)

That means you've lost an entire year of tax-free compound interest.

The sooner you make your contribution, the sooner your money starts compounding tax-free. Believe it or not, this can really make a difference. (OK, don't believe it. See if I care.)

Yes, It's Those Wild and Crazy Lunatics You've All Been Waiting For, Back by Popular Demand. Let's Have a Big Round of Applause for Sylvia and Willy!!!!

For example, Sylvia the Snake Charmer makes her RRSP contribution at the beginning of the year, when her snakes are asleep and she has nothing better to do anyway.

Slick Willy makes his RRSP contribution at the end of the year, having spend 11 months and 29 days combing his hair and polishing the toes of his cowboy boots.

Each invests $3,500 and earns 12% annually.

In 30 years, Sylvia will have $946,000.

Willy will have only $845,000. That's a difference of a hundred grand! (In fact, the higher the return on your investment, the bigger the difference.)

Sorry, Willy.

What's My Ultimate Goal?

My ultimate goal is to play the ukulele at Carnegie Hall with Nancy Sinatra.

But seriously, my ultimate financial goal is to accumulate as much as I can. Hey, I'm not greedy. What did you expect me to say?

If you want as much as you can accumulate when you retire, always make your maximum RRSP contribution.

Ask any of those old geezers at the lawn bowling club. They'll tell you that the retirement years come a lot sooner than any of us expects. And our retirement nest-egg looks more poached than scrambled (whatever that means).

More Tedious Math

Many people think that, because they have $100,000 saved up for retirement, they'll never have to worry about money again.

The trouble is, retirement is a lot more expensive than most people anticipate. If you have $100,000 earning 4% in the bank, and you want to remove $15,000 a year to cover your living expenses, how many years will it take to run out of money?

The answer: seven years.

At 10%, you could remove $15,000 for 10 years before your $100,000 ran out.

If you invest the money instead in some good quality mutual funds, you can earn 16% to 18% a year. At those rates, you can take out $15,000 a year for a long, long time.

Tips for Older Lawn Bowlers or I Want My Money Back

When the time comes to withdraw money from your RRSP, you have three basic choices:

➤ lump-sum withdrawals

➤ annuities, and

➤ RRIFs.

You must choose at least one of these options by the end of the year in which you turn age 69.

The Lump Sum (Not a Chinese Breakfast Cereal)

If you cash in all or part of your RRSP, then the amount you withdraw will be added to your income for that year and will be taxed as ordinary income.

Meanwhile, the financial institution that administers your RRSP will withhold a percentage of the money you withdraw and send it to Revenue Canada. This withheld money is simply a prepaid tax. The size of the withholding tax depends on the amount you withdraw.

➤ up to $5,000, you pay 10% withholding tax;

➤ $5,001 to $15,000, you pay 20%;

➤ over $15,000, you pay 30%.

For this reason, you're better off withdrawing $5,000 or less at a time. This allows you to keep more cash until you file your next tax return.

The Annuity (Not the Bippity-Boppity-Booity)

Let's get this straight:

The purchaser of an annuity is called the "Annuitant."

The company that sells the annuity is called the "Issuer."

The annuitant gives the issuer money in return for monthly income payments for life.

When you transfer your money from an RRSP to the issuer of an annuity, you don't have to pay tax on it. You pay tax only on the monthly payments you receive from the issuer.

Some people live with an annuitant. Some people live with a spouse. Some people live with both. They have great parties.

More Stuff You Don't Have to Know Until You Join the Lawn Bowling Club

There are basically three types of annuities: term certain, single life, and joint and last survivor.

➤ term certain annuities: you receive payments for a fixed term. If you die (possibly of boredom from reading this stuff) before the term is up, your estate receives the payments.

➤ single life annuities: the simplest type. You receive monthly payments for as long as you live.

➤ joint and last survivor life annuities: both you and your spouse (not him/her again!) continue to receive payments as long as either of you remains alive. (You don't have to prove you're alive. But it helps if you can move your lips.) The monthly payments are lower than they would be from a single life.

Up the Escalator

You can also choose an index, or escalating rate, annuity. This gives you monthly payments that never decrease, but may increase based on an interest-rate indicator. Your monthly payments will be lower than those of a straight life annuity during the early years, but the payments will eventually increase if and when interest rates rise.

Annuity Schmooity

With most annuities, you're locked in for life at the prevailing interest rate when you sign the contract. Insurance salesmen will tell you that people with annuities live longer than people without annuities. But if you buy one of these things when interest rates are low, you'll feel like killing yourself when inflation and interest rates start rising.

For example, say your fixed yearly payment is $10,000, and inflation rises to 5% a year. In 20 years, you'll need over $25,000 to maintain the purchasing power of today's $10,000. But since your payments are fixed, your purchasing power will fall.

To address this problem, some insurance companies like Sun Life sell cashable or retractable annuities. You can cash these annuities early, and then renegotiate your annuity once interest rates rise.

Go for the RRIF

Better still, forget about an annuity and go for a RRIF. (We cool dudes pronounce it like cliff.) A RRIF is a Registered Retirement Income Fund. For most people turning 69, a RRIF is the best choice.

At age 69, or sooner if you wish, you simply transfer your RRSP into a RRIF. You can own as many RRIFs as you like. In most cases, the institution holding your RRSP can set up a RRIF for you.

You can keep the same investments in your RRIF as you held in your RRSP. You can also continue to buy and sell investments within an RRIF.

The main difference is that, with the RRIF, you must withdraw a minimum amount of money each year, except the year in which you set it up. The money you withdraw from the RRIF will be taxed as income.

If You Really Want to Know, Here's How to Calculate Your Minimum RRIF Withdrawal (If You Make This Calculation In Your Head When You're 69 Years Old, You Get to Appear on Front Page Challenge)

If you're under 69, take the number 90, subtract your age, and divide the amount of the RRIF by the resulting number.

For instance: You're 65 years old. You've got $100,000 in your RRIF. To find out how much you have to withdraw per year, subtract 65 from 90, which leaves you with 25. Now divide $100,000 by 25: That comes to $4,000. That means you have to withdraw $4,000 in the first year of your RRIF.

Someone in the government actually thought about all this. If you want to know the rationale behind this calculation, talk to him/her. He/she's probably a spouse.

RRIF Calculations: Something to Look Forward to When the Lawn Bowling Ends

In each following year, you use the same calculation (90 minus your age, divided into the total market value of the RRIF).

When you reach age 69, you have to use a different calculation to determine the minimum withdrawal. Since RRIF payments are now received for life, a specific factor is used in calculating the minimum withdrawal. (You want to know how to make the calculation? What are you, nuts? Phone me. Better yet, phone your mother. She's looking for you.)

Facts for a Buck

More than 47% of Canadians over the age of 69 who were surveyed by Scotiabank in 1997 said they depend on their RRIF as a steady source of income for living expenses. About one-third felt concerned they might outlive their savings.

Almost the Last Word About RRIFs

Since RRIFs now last for life, they offer the best opportunity for deferring your taxes for the longest possible time.

Will You Still Need Me, Will You Still Feed Me?

Canadians live longer than ever these days. In fact, about 25% of men and 39% of woman who reach age 69 will live past 90. Each of them needs money to live. So will you.

The Ding-dong of Doom

You should designate your spouse or a financially dependent child as the beneficiary of your RRSP or RRIF. Then, if you die, your spouse can put the money tax-free into his or her RRSP or RRIF.

If there's no surviving spouse and the RRSP/RRIF funds are left to a financially dependent child or grandchild, the funds will be taxed at the child's marginal tax rate or used to purchase an annuity until the child turns 18.

If there's no surviving spouse and no children under age 18, the money goes to your estate and is reported as income on your final tax return. (That's right. First you die. Then you pay more taxes.)

I Wanna Make My Kid Smart

Most financial planners today recommend a Registered Education Savings Plan (RESP) as a vehicle for saving money for your child's education.

With a RESP, you can contribute up $1,500 a year, and no more than $31,500 over the life of the plan, for each child, grandchild, great-grandchild, etc. (Just how old are you, anyway?)

Unlike an RRSP, a RESP doesn't enable you to deduct your contributions from your taxable income. However, the income generated inside the plan can compound tax-free for up to 25 years.

You can either contribute to a group RESP or set up a self-directed RESP through a financial planner.

I Won't Grow Up. I Don't Wanna Go to School

If the RESP's beneficiary is a little wombat who refuses to go to school, you can transfer the funds to another beneficiary. But the new beneficiary has to be a full-time student attending a post-secondary institution.

Dead-end. Do Not Pass Go

If no beneficiary uses the RESP funds to attend a post-secondary institution, you can take back all the money that you contributed to the plan. But you lose all the tax-free compounding.

If you decide to get one of these plans, you better make sure somebody attends a post-secondary institution, or else you'll lose the opportunity to make money on your investments elsewhere.

The Better Way

A more prudent approach is to open a mutual fund in your child's name. You can either use the child's monthly tax-credit cheque or use your own money to invest in the child's name.

If you choose to invest the child's tax credit cheque, any money that the child earns should not be attributed back to the parents.

If you choose to give your child the money to invest, the rules are a little different.

Here Are the Rules. Don't Read Them If You're
a. Bored
b. Childless
c. Sick to Death of Tax-related Information and Ready to Jump Off a Bridge

For children under age 18, capital gains earned from money given to a child are not attributed back to the parents. Since most of a stock mutual fund's appreciation comes from capital gains, the majority of the gains will stay in the child's name and not be attributed back to you. However, interest and dividend income is attributed back to the contributing parent.

If you invest $1,000 each year into a good quality equity mutual fund, the 16% to 18% annual return your child will receive will turn that $1,000 annual contribution into $50,000 to $60,000 over a 15-year period. Over a 20-year period, it could easily turn into more than $100,000. That buys a lot of textbooks.

If I Can't Afford to Make My Maximum RRSP Contribution, Should I Borrow the Money to Invest?

People who don't have enough cash on hand to maximize their RRSP contributions should consider borrowing the money.

When we borrow money to invest outside of our RRSP, the interest on the loan is tax deductible. Interest on money borrowed for RRSPs, however, is not deductible.

But it can still be worth borrowing, as long as you can pay back the loan within a year. The longer it takes to pay back the money, the less benefit you'll receive.

Most financial institutions will lend you the money at the prime interest rate, providing you purchase your RRSP through that institution.

Last Dad-blasted Math Calculation, Honest

Let's say your maximum RRSP contribution is $8,000, and you have only $5,000 to invest.

If you borrow the other $3,000 from the bank and pay 7% interest on the loan, and you earn 7% on your RRSP investment, it really doesn't make much difference whether you borrowed to invest or not. You pay 7% and you earn 7%.

However, once you pay off the loan, your investment continues to compound tax-free.

The clincher, though, is the tax rebate. If you're in the 42% marginal tax bracket, that $3,000 contribution will provide you with a rebate of $1,260.

Now you're way ahead of the game. You can use that money to

help pay down the loan, buy a new stereo, take a trip to Florida, or buy another copy of this book for all your friends.

Read It and Reap

➤ Everyone age 69 or younger should own an RRSP.

➤ Try to make the maximum annual contribution to your RRSP.

➤ Try to contribute as early as you can in the year. Don't wait till the last minute.

➤ If your spouse earns less than you do, and you expect your spouse's income will be less than yours when you retire, consider a spousal RRSP.

➤ If you withdraw the funds before you retire, try to withdraw them when you're earning less income than usual, so you pay less tax.

➤ If you don't have cash to pay for your RRSP contribution, consider borrowing the money.

➤ Consider saving for your child's education by contributing to a mutual fund in your child's name.

➤ When you turn 69, don't buy an annuity unless interest rates are high. Otherwise, invest in a RRIF.

Chapter 10

Borrowing: Other People's Money

> ## In This Chapter
> ➤ The proper way to handle credit cards
> ➤ Different types of loans
> ➤ Understanding overdrafts

Act One, Scene One

"Neither a borrower nor a lender be." This isn't Shakespeare talking. This is one of his characters in *Hamlet* named Polonius, a purse-lipped lemon-sucking fuss-budget who's instructing his son, Laertes, about how he should behave when he journeys away from home. "Clean your fingernails, and don't forget to wash behind your ears, sblood," he might have added.

Of all people, Shakespeare knew the importance of borrowing. After all, he was in debt most of his life. If he hadn't been allowed to borrow money, he might never have had the time or the freedom to write his plays. And none of us would ever have had the dubious pleasure of writing a three-hour exam on the existential meaning of Hamlet's dilemma.

Borrowing and Growth and Stuff Like That

We've already seen, in our chapter on buying a house and in our chapter on buying stock, that the more money you invest, the more you stand to gain if your investment rises in value. (What? You don't remember those chapters. Forsooth. Hie ye forth and stand in yon corner with thine hands on thine head, you addle-pated codpiece.)

We've also seen that, for every dollar of your own, you can borrow another one, which lets you invest twice as much in a house or a stock.

In fact, if people couldn't borrow money, there would be half as many houses purchased and sold in a year; only a quarter of us would own a car; and there would be no streets to drive them on.

Cars, houses, roads, highways, sewers, bridges, buildings, streetlights, water mains, gas lines — just about everything that makes our cities and towns work is built on borrowed money.

If we couldn't borrow money, we'd still be wrapping ourselves in yak skins and sleeping under rocks.

So What, Uncle Mike?

So what? I'll tell you so what.

I'm not saying you should run out and borrow money every time you want to buy a case of beer. (The credit collection agencies would love you if you did. But they'd soon catch up to you. And then you wouldn't be allowed to borrow any more money, and you'd have to go hunting yaks.)

I'm just saying, as I've said before, that sometimes it pays to borrow.

If You Don't Borrow, You Can't Get a Credit Rating, and If You Don't Have a Credit Rating, You Can't Borrow, and If You Can't Borrow...

Here's a fine kettle of fish. How do you get a credit rating if you can't borrow money without one?

The answer? You get a credit card. Any kind will do, even one from a hardware or department store. Any idiot can get one of those, and usually does.

Use the card to make a small purchase. Then pay the balance as soon as you receive your statement.

Voila! Now you have a credit rating. Go forth and borrow your brains out. (No, no, just joking. Forget I said that.)

Moderation Pays the Highest Dividends

Using a credit card or borrowing money on a whim is the surest way to stay poor. Instead of investing money and earning 10% or 12%, you'll owe money and pay 15% or more until you pay it back. That's not an investment. That's dumb.

Free Money (Yell This on a Crowded Bus and See What Happens)

How would you like to borrow $2,000 to $5,000, interest-free? You can do it, but you'll need a credit card.

Using most credit cards, you can make a purchase on credit and not pay any interest until your bill comes due, in 30 days or more. At that point, all you have to do is pay off your balance in full. You just got a one-month interest-free loan.

Not So Free Money (Yell This on a Crowded Bus. Nothing Will Happen)

If you don't pay your bill in full when it comes due, the meter begins to run. On outstanding credit card balances, you pay interest rates of 16% or more. And you pay that rate on your entire balance. That's how credit card companies make money, from the 50% of card holders who don't pay their bills on time. Don't be one of them.

Bums, Losers, Deadbeats, Yobboes

If you miss a payment on your credit card, a little hunchbacked guy in a shiny grey suit with a pencil behind his ear scurries off to a filing cabinet in a basement six floors under the ground and pulls out a file with your name on it. Licking his pencil, he scribbles a little note on your file. From now on, your name is mud. That's MUD.

Later, when you go to a bank to borrow money for something

really important like a house or your child's new braces or a university education for your daughter, the bank manager will call the hunchbacked geezer in the grey suit to get your credit rating. The little git will say, "The name's MUD," and the bank manager will turn to you and say, "I'm so sorry, Rhonda, but we can't lend you any money today."

The lesson? Pay your bills on time, and your credit rating will take care of itself.

It's Never Too Soon

Credit cards come in handy. There's no doubt about it. When you've driven 300 km with your friend Timmy, who suddenly discovers that you're out of gas and he has no cash, a credit card will seem like gold as you pull into the gas station and fill 'er up. It will seem even more valuable when you rent a car and drive home, leaving Timmy behind to push his jalopy down the highway.

Credit card companies will issue cards to college and university students, in the hope that it might be the beginning of a long and profitable relationship. You might start out with a relatively low credit limit. But if you pay your bills on time, your credit limit will grow.

Chequing Out

The next best way to establish a credit rating is to open a chequing account at your local bank. Tell your bank representative that you want to establish a good credit rating. He'll give you advice on what to do.

Interesting!

When you take a cash advance with your credit card, interest begins to accumulate on the money from the day you withdraw it, not from the day you get your bill.

Likewise, if you make a partial payment on your outstanding bill after the due date, interest still accumulates on the entire balance up until you make the partial payment. For example, you purchase a new stereo system for $1,000 using your credit card. The due date passes and you can't pay more than the token interest payment. Then, two weeks later, you pay off $600, thinking that you will be charged interest only on the outstanding balance of $400.

Think again, Stan. You'll be charged interest on the full $1,000 up until the day the $600 payment was made. Interest then accrues on the outstanding amount.

Unless you pay off your balance on time and in full, you will be charged interest!

Credit Card Tidbits

➤ One-half of all people who own credit cards do not pay off their cards on time.

➤ A Canadian, taxed at a marginal rate of 42%, would have to purchase a $1,000 GIC that yields 26% a year to earn the equivalent of the annual payment on a $1,000 outstanding credit card balance. (If you can find a 26% GIC, I beg you, mamma, phone me. Oh, please phone me. Yo. Phone me this minute.)

➤ Instead of maintaining an outstanding credit card balance, get a low-interest credit card and pay off the higher-interest card with the lower-interest card (We've talked about this before, Len). Or take out a personal loan from a bank and pay down the outstanding balance. Using a bank loan at 9% or 10% to pay a credit card balance at 15% will save you about $50 a year on each $1,000 outstanding.

➤ Credit cards come with bells and whistles attached, such as frequent flyer points, collision insurance on car rentals, medical coverage during trips, and insurance on purchases that will fix or replace items that have been lost, stolen, or have broken. Most gold cards automatically provide extended warranty coverage.

➤ Some cards charge an annual fee, others don't. The ones that don't usually have no bells and whistles attached.

➤ If you ever find yourself unable to pay even the minimum monthly payment, notify the credit card company immediately. You'll can usually work out a payment plan.

➤ Many times the creditor will end up accepting less than the total amount, providing you can pay it in one lump sum payment.

➤ It's tempting to accumulate as many credit cards as we can, in case we need them on a rainy day. But when we apply for a mortgage, the bank or mortgage lender will add up all the outstanding credit provided by each card company and deduct the total from the mortgage available to us. In other words, if we have $10,000 in available credit with Visa, Mastercard, American Express, Canadian Tire, and Joe's Department Store, the bank will reduce the size of the mortgage that we can obtain by $10,000.

Installment Loans

If you borrow money to buy a car, a refrigerator, or a naugahyde couch and La-Z-Boy chair for your living room, you will likely take out an installment loan. With an installment loan, you borrow a specified amount of money and repay it in regular, specified amounts.

You make the payments according to a payment schedule. They can be weekly, bi-weekly, or monthly. Then you die.

Fixed or Variable

Installment loans come in two basic flavours: fixed-rate and variable-rate.

On a fixed-rate installment loan, you pay the same amount of interest with each payment for the life of the loan.

For example, if you borrow $10,000 at 10%, you'll pay $1,000 in interest over one year. Therefore, your total payments will be $11,000 or $916.66 per month.

Your lender can also calculate your interest payments on a declining basis. With each monthly payment, you reduce the outstanding principal. So the amount of interest that you pay, calculated as a percentage of the outstanding principal, decreases each month.

For example, let's say you take out a $10,000 loan at 10% and you pay it back over one year with monthly payments of $1,000. Your first

$1,000 payment will include $83.33 in interest (that's the monthly equivalent of 10% a year) plus a payment toward the principal of $916.67. That reduces the principal to $9,083.33, and the cycle starts again. The next payment includes interest of $75.69 (that's the monthly equivalent of 10% a year on $9,083.33) and payment toward the principal of $924.31. This continues for 11 months until you've paid off the loan. But at the end of the period, you've paid only $10,481.82 rather than $11,000. This is good for you, but not so good for the lender.

Variable-Rate Installment Loans

These are also called floating-rate loans. The interest on a floating-rate loan fluctuates in relation to the prime interest rate. If the prime rate goes up, so does the cost of the loan. If the prime rate falls, the interest rate on the loan falls too.

In most cases, the amount of your payment remains constant. But the proportion of your payment that goes toward the principal fluctuates according to the prevailing interest rate. If rates rise, less money goes to the principal; if rates fall, more goes to the principal. Obviously when rates are declining, you're better off with a variable-rate loan. If rates are rising, take a fixed-rate loan.

Demand Performance

A demand loan is a variable-rate loan that's payable on demand. (In fact, this applies to all loans. They're all payable on demand. But only some are actually called demand loans. The rest are called burdens or pains in the butt or other endearing terms.)

Demand loans usually have to be paid back in a short period of a few months. They're used most frequently for bridge financing, to tide you over short periods when you expect a lot of money tomorrow but you need a lot of money today.

For example, when you buy another house and pay for it with the proceeds from your current house, the dates when each transaction closes may not coincide. So the bank will lend you the money to pay for your new house until the purchaser of your old house forks over the dough.

Demand loans are also used frequently for investment purposes. The interest rates usually vary with the prime rate.

Have I Got a Line for You

If you have a good credit rating and a household income of at least $50,000, then you might qualify for a revolving personal loan called a personal line of credit (PLC). A financial institution will check out your credit rating and make sure you're the honest upstanding citizen that you say you are, and then authorize you to write cheques on your PLC up to a specified limit.

A PLC carries a much lower rate of interest than a credit card. If you guarantee your PLC with equity in your house, the interest rate will be even lower. But it does come at a cost.

To guarantee a PLC with your house, you can usually use up to 70% of the value of your house, after subtracting outstanding mortgages. So if your house is worth $250,000 and you have a mortgage of $100,000, you can use 70% of the remaining $150,000 as collateral against your PLC.

Repayment of a PLC balance is made at a floating rate of interest, and you usually have to make a minimum monthly payment.

A PLC gives you ready access to cash at a reasonable interest rate, if you need it.

Looney Lingo

A borrower offers COLLATERAL to a lender as protection. If the borrower cannot repay a loan, the lender can take the collateral in place of the outstanding amount. Financial institutions prefer collateral in the form of property, usually your house, especially for a PLC. You can also use paper securities such as GICs, CSBs, and even mutual funds. But you can't use your RRSPs for collateral.

MOVABLE ASSETS such as cars, trailers and 40-kilogram stuffed tunas can be used as collateral to secure a loan. If you pledge your car as collateral against a loan to buy it, and then default on the loan payments, the bank will take possession of your car. Tunas are trickier.

Doodling in the Margins: Margin Accounts

Most brokerage firms, including discount brokers, will allow you to open a margin account. With a margin account, you can borrow money from the brokerage to buy securities. The brokerage will limit the

DOLLARS AND SENSE
$¢$¢$¢$¢ Your broker may tell you that by combining your own re-sources with money borrowed on margin from the brokerage, you can increase the value of your investments much more quickly. He can talk. He doesn't have to repay the loan. You should borrow on margin only when you have the resources to repay the loan quickly. Even then it's risky and you should proceed with caution.

amount you can borrow to a percentage of your total portfolio and monitor your account to make sure you don't exceed your limit. If you do, the brokerage will ask you to repay at least a portion of the loan. And there's the rub: If the value of your securities takes a tumble — as it will during turbulent periods in the market — you'll have to repay your loan. Where will you get the money, honey?

Understanding Overdrafts

When you write a cheque and you don't have enough money in your bank account to cover it, the bank will send the cheque back to you, the person to whom you gave the cheque in the first place will get mad at you, and you'll have to pay a $20 fee for all the brouhaha.

To avoid this type of situation, you should consider overdraft pro-tection. Now if you write a cheque without enough money in your ac-count to cover it, your overdraft protection will ensure that it still goes through the system. Overdrafts carry a high rate of interest, equal to or higher than a credit card. And they come with a limit ranging from $50 to $5,000, depending upon your personal financial situation.

The bank also applies a service charge, usually $1 a month. And you usually have to repay the overdraft within 60 days.

Read It and Reap

➤ If people couldn't borrow money, there would be half as many houses purchased and sold in a year; only a quarter of us would own a car; and there would be no streets to drive them on.

165

➤ Credit card companies make money from the 50% of card holders who don't pay their bills on time. Don't be one of them.

➤ Installment loans come in two basic flavours: fixed-rate and variable-rate.

➤ A personal line of credit, secured by a second mortgage on your house, carries a much lower rate of interest than a credit card.

NOW!
$92.00

NOW!
$81.00

Chapter 11

Inflation: Here Today, Sort of Here Tomorrow

In This Chapter

➤ What is inflation?

➤ What causes it and how do we measure it?

➤ Is it really bad?

➤ Hyperinflation

➤ Do interest rates have to go up?

➤ The effect of inflation and interest rates on the dollar

➤ Some boring economic history

➤ The big crash

➤ How much is your dollar worth?

What Is Inflation?

When prices go up, the purchasing power of your money falls. That, in a nutshell, is inflation.

Here's an example: In 1970, you could buy six chocolate bars, three bags of potato chips, and two packs of hockey cards for $1. Today, $1 buys a single chocolate bar. That's inflation.

Inflation in 225 Words

Here's what happens in a world where everything works. If you don't live in such a world, don't blame me. Neither do I. But at least we know it. (People like Madonna don't.)

For a number of reasons that we won't go into now, the government, through the Bank of Canada, prints a certain amount of money. Ideally, this money keeps its value. In fact, the money loses value almost as soon as it comes off the press. (If you really want to know why this happens, call the Bank of Canada and ask someone to explain it to you.)

When the value of your money falls, you need more money to buy the same amount of goods.

When you need more money, you ask your employer. Your employer, of course, says, "Sure, Trixie, whatever you want." And you get a raise.

To pay your increased salary, your employer increases the price of his product. Now your employer's customers find they need more money to buy the same amount of products or services as they bought last year. They go to their employers and ask for more money. And, of course, their employers give it to them.

Meanwhile, the government raises taxes, not only because money in general is worth less and the government needs more, but because that's what governments do.

The sum total of all this is inflation.

Supply and Demand (There's Exciting Stuff Coming, Honest)

Here's the economic principle of supply and demand: When supply is greater than demand, prices fall; when demand is greater than supply, prices rise.

You may know this already. If you do, go to the next section or turn on your stereo and slam dance for a few minutes while I explain this more clearly.

A True Story About Beach Balls

The Unbelievable Beach Ball Company has 15 beach balls, but can find only 11 people to buy them. It's the beginning of summer, and the

Unbelievable Beach Ball Company's managers all consider quitting and joining another company. Meanwhile, the supply of beach balls is greater than the demand. Why would any of the 11 people who want one pay full price? In fact, none of them does.

Instead, they start to haggle and negotiate with the president of the Unbelievable Beach Ball Company, Chet Unbelievable. Under great pressure, the company finally drops its price.

A couple of people, eager to get to the beach before December, each buy a ball. The other nine people wait, knowing the price may drop even further, because, even though there are only 13 balls left, there are now only nine people who want one.

Months pass. November comes. The beach closes. Chet Unbelievable takes a trip with his family — wife Chaquita, son Chub, and daughter Cherry Blossom — to Lake Okeefenokee, Florida, where Cherry Blossom falls in love with a lifeguard, who is actually an undercover agent for the Cuban Liberation Army. Chub develops a rash from drinking piña colada and has to stay indoors, wrapped in green garbage bags. Meanwhile, Chet's company stands firm. The price of beach balls does not drop any further.

Suddenly, in January, Chet's company receives an urgent message from Argentina. The Buenos Aires All-Star Beach Ball Association (BAAS-BBA) needs beach balls. "Help," says the message. "Need beach balls real quick. Will pay top peso for 300 balls."

Now the Unbelievable Beach Ball Company's 13 balls are in big demand. ("Nyorg, nyorg, nyorg," chuckles President Chet.) The company doubles the price of its balls. The BAASBBA buys the balls. Chet Unbelievable makes a huge profit. His son, Chub, steals the family Mercedes. Many amazing things happen. The nine people who waited for the price to fall further go home.

The end.

Here's What Really Happens

During prosperous periods, such as 1983 to 1989, people buy stuff like there's no tomorrow. To pay for them, they borrow money. With everybody borrowing money, the demand for money increases.

Money, like beach balls, rises and falls in price depending on supply and demand. When the demand for money increases, the supply goes down and the price goes up.

Inflation has been low for the past couple of years while governments in Canada try to get their deficits under control. But the economy is getting healthy again, profits are up, and people are beginning to spend. Watch for inflation to raise its ugly head in a year or two.

How Much for That C-Note in the Window?

Question: What is the price of money?

Answer: The interest rate you pay to borrow it.

You Can Bank on It

While we shop till we drop, bankers, led by the Bank of Canada, push interest rates higher and higher. They know that, sooner or later, we'll stop borrowing and start saving.

Finally they make interest rates so high that people stop borrowing. Anyone with some money sticks it in a savings account or a GIC or a Canada Savings Bond, where it earns a high rate of interest and pays for Uncle Gumby's new teeth.

The rest of us fork out huge gobs of money in interest on our mortgages, car loans, and credit cards, hoping interest rates will go down again before we jump out the window.

Sale, Sale, Sale

Of course, now that we've stopped buying things, the retailers who sell them and the companies who make them don't make any money. They go broke. All the stuff they have on their shelves and in their warehouses goes on sale. Supply goes up, prices fall. But nobody has any money, so who cares?

When people stop buying, they also stop borrowing. The companies that sell money — which we call banks — drop their prices, hoping to attract customers.

How to Act Like a Lemming

When the price of money falls, the interest rates on savings accounts and Canada Savings Bonds go down, too.

If they have any money, people take it out of the bank and spend it. Once again, they start buying things and borrowing to pay for them. And the whole cycle starts over.

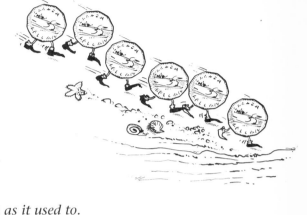

Looney Lingo

INFLATION is an economic term used to describe the rising prices of goods and services. As a result of increased prices, the purchasing power of our money falls, because a dollar will no longer buy as much as it used to.

The Consumer Price Index (CPI)

In the front of a book on gardening, you'll find a list of topics inside. This list is called an index.

The Consumer Price Index, also known as the CPI (not to be confused with the CIA or the FBI or the "Sea-Green Bundle-Buggy" by Leo Tolstoy) is an index, too. But instead of describing chapters in a book, the CPI describes different parts of our economy.

The Nine Chapters of the CPI

If you found the CPI at the front of a book, it would list a whole bunch of things, organized in nine major groups:

1. food
2. housing
3. clothing
4. transportation
5. health & personal care
6. recreation-reading & education
7. tobacco & alcohol
8. food purchased from restaurants, and
9. all items excluding food

These major groups are then divided further into specific goods, such as mortgages, polyester pants, and ground beef, to name just a few.

This Is a Job for Super-phone-man

Each month agents of Statistics Canada contact retail and service businesses across the country to find out how much they're charging for the prices of 300 different items.

The cost of these items is then compared to their cost in the same month, one year earlier.

What's It All Mean, Mister Mike?

Most newspapers carry monthly CPI data. These data indicate trends in inflation. For example, in November 1997 Statistics Canada reported the September CPI to be up 1.6% from what it was a year earlier.

But data, like politicians, can sometimes be misleading. In 1994, StatsCanada reported the January CPI to be up 1.3% over the previous year. But the February CPI was up only 0.2% over the previous year. It was the largest one-month drop in the CPI since June 1959, and people began to worry that the country would descend quickly into an economic bog.

But the month-to-month decline was directly related to a 38% cut in cigarette prices, which resulted from lower taxes. If cigarette prices had remained unchanged, the February CPI would have been 1.5%.

Nevertheless, the CPI is the most widely watched inflationary gauge. Not only does it let the government know whether or not the economy needs to be stimulated or restrained, it also affects social insurance benefits, taxes, and negotiations between businesses and unions regarding wage increases.

Don't Worry, Peaches, Everything's Under Control

When the CPI rises an average of 2% a year, the inflation rate is low. If it rises by 2% to 4%, then the inflation rate is average.

When the CPI rises at a rate above 5%, central bankers become concerned. (Some day I'll tell you more about central bankers. But not today.)

Above 6%, and interest rates start rising.

The Goldilocks Economy

Inflation can be too high. It can also be too low. When it's too high, people can't borrow, and they stop spending.

When there's no inflation at all, it means there's no demand for money. The economy has stopped growing.

With moderate inflation, the economy grows steadily. It grows slowly but surely. It grows moderately. It grows not too hot, not too cold, but just right.

OK, who's been sleeping in my bed?

Trick Question: What Causes Inflation?

There are as many theories about the causes of inflation as there are economists to spout them.

Here are two of the more popular ones. They even have names:

➤ Demand Pull Inflation and

➤ Cost Push Inflation

I'll bet you're waiting for me to explain what these theories are all about. Forget it. I'll give you my own instead. (It has a better name.)

Captain Mike's Theory of Inflation

The real cause of inflation: too many dollars chasing too few goods.

The Politics of Inflation

Inflation almost always begins with a politician, and usually more than one.

Before they're elected, politicians promise to lower taxes, raise old age pensions, create jobs, eliminate unsightly wrinkles, and put justice and mercy back into the school system where it belongs.

Then they get elected. To fulfill at least some of their pre-election blatherings, they need money. They can't just raise taxes, although they can try, and they usually do. More often, they instruct the Bank of Canada to create more money. *Voila*, instant dough!

At first, this new money creates a sense of prosperity. People have more to spend, so they buy cars, televisions, and CD players. Manufacturers' profits rise, so they invest in new plants and equipment and hire new employees to run it all.

Then prices begin to rise, and that extra cash starts buying less and less.

Yes, folks, there you have it. Inflation rides again. Too many dollars chasing too few goods. And don't say that Uncle Mike didn't warn you.

Nothing Up My Sleeve

If you want to get technical, the value of goods seldom rises at all. People value a hammer today just as much as they valued it in 1960.

What changes is the value of your dollar. That's why prices have risen since 1960 by over 300%. And why Aunt Millie can get away with saying, "Why when I was your age, a quarter was a lot of money."

Looney Lingo

DEMAND PULL INFLATION is based on the premise that increased demand for goods and services will pull up prices.

COST PUSH INFLATION is based on the premise that manufacturers will raise their prices to make a profit if the cost of producing goods and services goes up.

DOLLARS AND SENSE
¢ $ ¢ $ ¢ $ ¢

Who benefits from low inflation? The government. Governments borrow more money than anyone else in the country. When they can borrow your money and pay you half as much as they paid last year, they're happy.

Who benefits from high inflation? The government. When they can borrow money at low rates this year and then pay it back next year with dollars that are worth less than the dollars they borrowed, they're happy.

How Much Money Is Enough?

Money is like an IOU from the government. It's supposed to represent a claim on some tangible asset.

The amount of money in the economy should reflect its tangible assets, such as gold. Between the First and Second World Wars, however, most governments stopped basing their money supply on the gold stored in their vaults. Now money represents something less tangible.

IOU Blues

Until 1967, Canadian paper money carried the words, "Will pay to the bearer on demand."

Those words remained on our currency because, in the deep, dark, distant past, a person could actually walk into a bank, hand the teller a bill and ask for the equivalent amount of gold.

Those days ended in 1940, when Canada stopped backing its currency with gold. But the words remained on the currency because:

    a. no one wanted to go through every bill in circulation and scratch them out;

    b. they contained a secret code known only to Mackenzie King and John Diefenbaker;

    c. read backwards quickly six times they said "God runs a Dairy Queen in Sackville."

Sorry, Charlie

For whatever reason, those words preserved the illusion that our money was actually backed by gold. But if you'd walked into a bank with a $20 bill and demanded your gold, you'd have been lucky to receive two tens and a free rain bonnet.

Today our paper currency carries the words, "This note is legal tender."

Money and the Emperor's New Clothes

Today our money isn't backed by gold, it isn't backed by hockey sticks, and it isn't backed by baby seals or tractors. In fact, it's not backed by anything but our potential to work hard, make money, and die a little richer than we were when we started.

The only reason our money is worth anything is because people think that it's worth something. If everyone accepts our money as valuable, it's valuable.

Currency not backed by any tangible asset is called fiat money.

The Rich Get Richer

People living on fixed incomes — pensions, interest on savings, welfare, social security payments, disability, etc. — get hit the hardest by inflation. That's because, as the value of their money declines, they continue to receive the same amount. In inflationary periods, their standard of living falls.

For example, if you're living on the interest from an 8% government bond when inflation is running at 8%, then the real value of your income is holding steady. If inflation hits 9%, and you're still getting 8%, you're actually losing money. In addition, if you decide to sell prior to maturity, you'll have to take a big loss. (That's why you should avoid bonds during periods of rising inflation. But of course, you already know that, having read the chapter on bonds.)

Business Suffers, Too

Individuals aren't the only ones hurt by inflation. Inflation also hits businesses that sell consumer products.

During the early phases of inflation, consumer spending increases as disposable income rises. However, once inflation gets going, and the bills get bigger, people realize that their money doesn't go as far as it used to, and they refuse to pay those high prices.

Meanwhile, many companies can't raise their prices. They have to compete against other companies that were better managed or luckier, and against imports from other countries. But their costs keep rising, and their profits keep going down.

During periods like this, you should avoid buying stock in consumer-oriented companies such as retailers and manufacturers of consumer goods.

What Is Hyperinflation?

Sometimes prices increase at such an accelerating rate that people can't store enough of it today to buy a loaf of bread tomorrow. So they lose all confidence in the purchasing power of their money.

When people fear that their money will become worthless, they rush out to spend it while they still can. But because it's depreciating so fast, businesses refuse to accept it. This is called hyperinflation.

Hyperinflation occurred in Germany in the 1920s. It occurred more recently in places like Israel and Argentina. It's unlikely to occur in Canada.

Why Not Canada?

Hyperinflation in Canada? You must be joking. There would have to be a civil war. A revolution. Or a government collapse. Heard any good Quebec jokes lately?

A Wee Diversion (If You Don't Like History, Take a Wee Hike)

In the early 19th century, individual banks issued their own money in the form of bank notes. People would take gold to their local bank for safekeeping. In return, the bank would issue them bank notes, which they could convert back into gold at any time.

These bank notes were literally as good as gold, and businesses accepted them as legitimate currency.

To cover withdrawals, each bank had to keep a certain amount of gold on hand. But few people conducted business transactions in gold, preferring bank notes instead. So a bank could issue bank notes with a total value higher than the gold in its vaults.

Nevertheless, banks maintained a predetermined ratio of gold to bank notes, just in case someone decided to cash in his notes.

Our Wee Story Continues

When people wanted to borrow money, the bank would issue bank notes and charge interest on the loan. But the bank could lend money only in proportion to the gold in its vault.

In the old days, just as in modern times, the demand for loans increased during times of prosperity. Banks raised their interest rates to reflect the increasing demand. As usual, when interest rates went high enough, people stopped spending.

When people stop spending, the economy goes into a sharp, but short-lived recession. Stocks that have been bid up in price come down to fair value. Interest rates fall once again. Borrowing becomes more attractive, and banks can make a profit. Businesses restructure, and the economy gets ready to begin another expansionary phase.

Have I Got a Deal for You

Before the 20th century, most banks set their own interest rates, depending on the supply and demand for money. Since there was a direct connection between supply and demand, the economy acted accordingly. Interest rates — the price of money — remained relatively stable, and there was little speculation. But people didn't like watching banks make money apparently for doing nothing. What else is new?

Then in 1914, the Federal Reserve was formed in the United States. (The Federal Reserve is comparable to the Bank of Canada, which began operations in 1935.) Among other things, the Federal Reserve relieved individual banks of the chore of printing money, calculating ratios of gold to currency, and all the other boring stuff that central bankers now do.

The Federal Reserve's original purpose was to keep the price of money low. Credit and interest rates were no longer to be determined by the rules of supply and demand. Instead, all this would now be decided by the Federal Reserve. Easy credit became the new rule of the day, unless the Federal Reserve decided otherwise.

Here Comes the Crash

The government figured that if it took control of money and credit away from the greedy, profit-oriented bankers, then it could control investment and guarantee continuous economic prosperity.

In 1914, the interest rate set by the Federal Reserve on its money was 6%. By 1922, it was down to 4.5%, and did not rise higher until 1928. Naturally banks kept their interest rates low, too. Anyone depositing money with a bank received little more than 2%. And people could borrow money for little more than 5%.

To get a better return on their money, people began looking elsewhere for investment opportunities. And those wily guys with the pencil-thin mustaches saw them coming. Unsophisticated geeks invested in things like the Brooklyn Bridge; and the amazing process that turns bicycle spokes into gold; and the machine that reverses the aging process; and that elixir that brings dead people back to life.

In fact, by the end of 1928, people were speculating in just about anything that had a stock certificate attached to it. And they were borrowing money to do it.

At that time, margin requirements were only about 10%. To buy $1,000 worth of stock, you needed just $100. To double your original investment of $100, the stock had to appreciate by only 10%. (I know, I know. We've already done this. Don't worry. You don't have to go back to math class.)

Guess What Happens Next?

With interest rates so low, money started pouring into the stock market. The greatest stock market advance in history resulted. Between 1921 and 1929, the stock market rose by almost 500%.

In 1927, a warning sign appeared when the economy shrunk slightly. But the Federal Reserve paid no attention. Instead, it kept priming the pump, pouring more paper money into the system to prevent a possible shortage in bank reserves.

DOLLARS AND SENSE
$¢$¢$¢$¢

From 1929 to 1932, stock prices fell so low that many investors had to keep their stock certificates piled in cartons in the basement. At least that's what my grandfather told me, and he was one smart investor. He wasn't affected at all by the crash of '29. He lost all his money in '28.

By 1928, the stock market was seriously overvalued, and people were still borrowing furiously to invest in it. But the government ignored all the warning signals until May 18, 1928. Then, to put the brakes on all this mad borrowing, it raised interest rates three consecutive times. They finally settled at 6% on August 9, 1929. But it was too little, too late.

The Dow Industrials hit a record high of 381.17 on September 3, 1929, and then started heading south at an ever-increasing rate, until the big crash on October 29, 1929. That was just the beginning of the worst stock market decline in history. By July 8, 1932, the Dow had tumbled 89% to a low of 41.22 .

Why Do Interest Rates Have to Go Up?

Many people cannot understand why the Bank of Canada or the U.S. Federal Reserve have to raise interest rates. If lower interest rates prompt us to take our money out of the bank and spend it, why not keep interest rates artificially low all the time and have a continuous economic boom?

That would make sense if each part of the economy worked in a coordinated fashion. If, for example, we could be certain that most people had jobs when prices went up, or that companies could buy steel and oil and other raw materials at stable prices, year after year, to meet the demand for their products, then we'd have a continuous economic boom. This is called a planned economy. It's been tried before. It gave us the 35-year economic boom in Cuba. And the 80-year boom in the former Soviet Union. Hey, those were some booms.

In fact, planned economies never work. The laws of supply and demand are much more efficient at regulating periods of boom and bust. They can be brutal. But they're based on reality, not on the intellectual doodlings of some old geezer with a beard.

Under the law of supply and demand, interest rates rise when the demand for money increases, during periods of economic expansion, for example. But if the demand for money increases while the government keeps interest rates artificially low, then demand far exceeds supply. Companies can't keep up. People stand around with wads of cash in their hands but nothing to spend it on. Insanity prevails. They eat their money, run naked into the street, and lie down under garbage trucks.

But Seriously...

When the government raises interest rates, it is applying monetary policy. Used alone it is quite effective at curbing inflation.

When the government raises taxes, it's applying fiscal policy.

Through fiscal policy, the government raises taxes so that consumers have less money to spend on frivolous items like candy bars and edible underwear and disposable watches. This money is called disposable income.

The government figures that if people don't have so much, then they won't spend as much. It's not brilliant thinking, but hey, we're dealing with the government here.

The government can also reduce its own spending by discontinuing public projects. Once again, people who rely on these projects for their income will have less money to spend. And businesses will have to lower prices.

Governments try to maintain the economy on a steady course. It wants to avoid rapidly rising inflation. And it wants to avoid rapidly falling prices, (also known as deflation).

Much of this balancing act has been delegated to the central banks, namely the Bank of Canada and the U.S. Federal Reserve.

Sis, Boom, Bust (You've Read a Lot of This Already in a Different Form. But What the Heck. Read It Again. What Else Do You Have to Do?)

After the economic boom comes the bust, often called a recession. During a recession, demand falls. So do production and employment.

When people lose their jobs, they bring less money home, or none at all. So they spend less.

This cycle continues until people feel more confident in their future (usually when they find another job). Then they start buying again.

The Formal Definition of Recession

Economists tell us that it takes two or more consecutive periods of three months apiece (also called a quarter. Three months equal one-quarter of a year, get it? Those economists. What a bunch of guys, eh?) when the nation's total output (also called Gross Domestic Product, because it's production, it's domestic, and it's gross) falls for the economy to be in a recession. There. Nothing to it.

This Is Depressing

A recession that gets off the leash is called a depression. In a depression, no one has a job. People walk around in the streets looking dazed and grey and wearing baggy suit pants and T-shirts. Sort of like downtown Toronto today.

Consumer demand falls. (What else is new? No one has any money.) So does investor confidence. (How can you feel confident in an economy that lets people sleep in the streets?) Trade and investment tumble. (Hey, I'll trade you a bushel of coal for that 20-storey building.)

Here Come Those Foreign Scalawags

To invest in Canada, foreign investors buy Canadian dollars and use them to buy shares in Canadian companies.

When Canada's inflation rate is low relative to the rate in other countries, foreign investors feel confident about buying Canadian stocks. They know that their money will hold its value. This increases demand for our dollar and strengthens it.

When the inflation rate in Canada is high relative to other countries, foreign investors lose confidence in Canadian stocks and invest in other countries. This weakens our dollar.

Oy, Monsieur, Check Out Those Rates

When Canadian interest rates are high relative to rates in other countries, foreign investors, seeking the highest yields, convert their own currency into Canadian dollars and use them to buy Canadian bonds. This strengthens our dollar.

When Canadian interest rates are low, investors sell their Canadian dollars and buy foreign bonds. This weakens our dollar.

DOLLARS AND SENSE
$¢$¢$¢$¢ For most Canadians, a recession occurs when your next door neighbour gets laid off. A depression occurs when you get laid off.

It's Looney at the Top

Over the past 25 years, the Canadian dollar has gone up and down like the frequent flyer of currencies. It hasn't always been that way.

Between 1939 and 1946, the Canadian dollar was fixed at 90.9 U.S. cents.

In 1946, the fixed rate was raised to US$1.

Only in 1950 did the government let the value of the dollar be determined by the open market. At that time, the Canadian dollar was in such demand that the market valued it at US$1.05 by the late 1950s, where it remained until 1961.

This was just fine for people who bought things in other countries and brought them back to Canada. The dollar bought a lot of Italian spaghetti and Swiss cuckoo clocks. But it wasn't such a good deal for

182

Canadian companies that wanted to sell things in other countries. (And most of our big companies do.) Who'd pay $1.05 for a pile of Canadian wood that you could buy somewhere else for $1?

Under pressure, the government decided that enough was enough. In 1962, it fixed the Canadian dollar at 92.5 U.S. cents.

But once again, in 1970, the government changed its mind and left the exchange rate to free-market forces to determine.

One Last Math Problem to Leave Your Brain in a Knot

If the newspaper says the Canadian dollar is worth 75 U.S. cents, why does the bank charge $1.35 to buy a U.S. dollar? Don't you just subtract 0.75 from 1.00 to get .25 (which equals a quarter) and add it to one dollar?

Boy, am I glad you didn't build the space shuttle.

To calculate the exchange rate, take your calculator and figure out how many times 0.75 can be divided into 1. That will tell you how many U.S. dollars there are in one Canadian dollar.

The actual calculation looks like this:

If US$0.75 = C$1, then US$1 = $1 divided by $0.75 = C$1.33.

Scary, huh?

> **LEARN AND EARN**
>
> You can find up-to-the-minute data on the rate of inflation and other exciting stuff through the Internet. At www.statcan.ca, for example, you can check on housing starts, the CPI, and the price of oil. At www.fin.gc.ca you can find data from the Department of Finance. Banks operate economic web sites as well. Scotiabank's can be reached at www.scotiabank.ca. (Now you can have all these web site addresses tattooed on your chest ... and your shoulders, down your back, and along your right leg.)

The additional two cents ($1.35 - $1.33 = 2 cents) is the amount that the bank charges to convert your money into another currency.

Read It and Reap

> ➤ Inflation is an economic condition characterized by rising prices for goods and services.

➤ The main cause of inflation is too many dollars chasing too few goods.

➤ Inflation is measured by the consumer price index (CPI).

➤ Individuals living on fixed incomes like pensions are most affected by inflation.

➤ When inflation rises so much that people lose confidence in the purchasing power of their money and lug it around town in wheelbarrows, hyperinflation occurs.

➤ The Bank of Canada and the Federal Reserve are responsible for adjusting interest rates to stimulate or restrain economic growth.

➤ When central bankers want to stop inflation, they raise interest rates. When inflation stops occurring at all, they lower interest rates.

➤ Bonds are not a wise purchase when inflation's rising.

➤ If our inflation rate is higher than other countries', our dollar weakens.

➤ During periods of rising inflation, the best place to put your money is in wealth in the ground, like gold, oil, and real estate.

Chapter 12

Risk: Mountain Climbing, Bungee-jumping, Hang Gliding, Investing, and Other Forms of Risk

In This Chapter

➤ The risks of investing

➤ Become educated first

➤ Inflation risk

➤ Re-investment risk

➤ Tax risk

➤ Stock market risk

➤ Financial genius risk

Me Invest in Stocks? No Way, Jose

Many people don't want to take the risk of investing their money anywhere other than a nice, safe bank account. Even a GIC scares them a little.

In fact, only about one in 10 Canadians ever invests directly in the stock or bond markets. (Indirectly, a lot more do — whether they like it or not — because the administrators of their pension plans invest their money for them.)

Life Is Risk

There's an old saying: We all want to go to heaven, but none of us wants to die. We take the same attitude when it comes to investing. We all want to double our money, but none of us wants to take a financial risk.

Lighten up, Alice. If you didn't take any risks at all, you'd never lace up those big black orthopedic shoes and take a walk to the corner store for a package of bunion pads. Life is risk.

Long on Risk, Short on Chance

Here's how I see the difference between risk and chance:

Stock car racing is inherently risky. There's always the risk that you'll drive into a wall at 150 kph, roll over three times, and ride your crankshaft into the sunset.

But stock car drivers understand the risks involved in their sport. And within this context, they don't take chances. Unlike many drivers on the less risky but more dangerous highways of our nation, they think about what they're doing. And most of the time, they do it without killing themselves.

In the midst of all that risk, they actually drive safely.

When it comes to our financial security, we operate within a general context of risk. There's political risk, for example, and interest-rate risk, and currency risk — when the Canadian dollar goes up and down like a yo-yo. These risks affect us even if we keep our money in a sock in the basement behind the Tide.

But within the context of these risks, a good investor, like a good driver, can operate safely.

There's No Sure Thing

No investment is risk-free. Our opportunity for gain is always balanced by our risk of loss. But we can calculate our risk and, when we do, we can see that an investment in a stock or mutual fund presents far less risk of losing money than an investment in a lottery ticket. Guess which investment attracts more suckers — er, investors?

We have to learn how to master risk, not become its slave. People who measured their risk and acted on it made a fortune during the crashes of 1929 and 1987. Likewise, investors who financed real estate deals prior to the German hyperinflation of 1923 ended up paying off their properties with pennies on the dollar. Not all of them were just lucky.

Investors who understand risk can make a profit, whether the market goes up or down.

A Perfect Balance: Nothing Ventured, Nothing Gained

The greater the risk, the greater the potential reward. We just have to determine our tolerance for risk. To do that, it helps if we can recognize the different types of risk that we encounter as we invest. Not all risks act the same. Like a convention of scary monsters, each one has its own schtick. Some of them eat you quickly. Others like to suck the juices out of you slowly and agonizingly. Still others sneak up behind you and smother you, and some fall on you from a great height. (Come to think of it, what am I doing in a place like this?)

Monster in a Sock

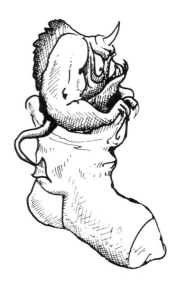

If you stuff your money in a sock and bury it in the ground, it will lose its value. So will your money. Nyuk, nyuk, nyuk. (Read the chapter on inflation if you don't believe me.)

Inflation averages about 4% a year. It dropped to around 2% in the late 1990s, but just wait till we head into the next century. At 4%, the cost of living doubles every 18 years. This is called purchasing power risk.

How to avoid it? Most Canadians put their money in a government-insured, guaranteed investment certificate or GIC. This provides a fixed rate of return. It's predictable and safe.

But it's not entirely risk-free. Say you invest

$10,000 in a GIC that pays 6%, when inflation is running at 4%. If you subtract the rate of inflation from the yield on the GIC, you end up with 2%. (Don't worry, I've done the math on this one. It took me all night, but I did it.)

At 2% a year, you'll double your money every 36 years. In three centuries, you'll be able to afford a bigger house.

Meanwhile, if inflation goes up to 7%, you actually lose 1% of the value of your investment every year.

Well, at least your money's safe.

Investments that provide a variable rate of return, such as common stocks and real estate, usually respond positively to inflation and let you stay ahead of the game. (See our chapter on stocks. See Spot run. Go, Spot, go, you dog, you.)

Monster Surprise

When inflation slows down, interest rates fall. If your fixed-interest investment such as a GIC or Canada Savings Bond matures at this point, and you re-invest it, you have to take a cut in your rate of return.

During 1981 and 1982, the rate of interest on Canada Savings Bonds fell overnight from 19.5% to 10.5%.

People like senior citizens, whose fixed income was derived from their investments in CSBs, found their incomes cut in half.

To protect yourself against interest rate risk, you should keep some of your money in short-term investments, like a money market fund, so you'll have the cash on hand to invest when rates start to rise again.

Monsters in Power

When a nation becomes politically unstable, the value of investments in the nation goes down. That's because the political risk of turmoil , revolution, long-haired weirdoes in power, radical changes in tax policy, and other hubbubs and brouhahas becomes more serious.

➤ In March, 1994, the leading candidate for the Mexican presidency, Luis Colosio, was assassinated. In the following two weeks, the Mexican stock market fell 10%.

➤ In 1939, German troops marched through Czechoslovakia. Stock prices around the world fell 20%.

➤ In 1974, the Watergate scandal caused stocks to tumble 28%.

For investors who understand the nature of political risk, these unpredictable occurrences present excellent buying opportunities.

The Change Monster

Things change. Life goes on. And then we die. (I really exhausted myself coming up with that one. Ludwig Wittgenstein couldn't have said it better.) Insightful investors can often profit from changes in society.

From our concern for the environment, for example, new companies have evolved that have made money for their investors.

From our concern for our health, drug companies and private medical services have profited, along with their investors.

It pays to read the newspaper. (If I keep coming up with these zingers, I might get a job writing for a fortune cookie company.)

Monsters in Flight

When the value of the dollar falls from 89¢ U.S. to 70¢ U.S. in two years, we've just experienced the effects of currency risk.

When we hand a bank teller a crisp new Canadian $100 bill and get back $65 in ugly wrinkled U.S. dollars, currency risk has descended upon us again.

When you invest in Greece, and the Greek drachma suddenly loses its value because some hairy-faced general has threatened to occupy the Parthenon, you get creamed when you sell your investment and convert the proceeds back into Canadian dollars.

There are ways to protect yourself against currency risk. (Maybe we'll discuss them in my next book. I think I'll call it *War and Peace*.) But for now, it's important simply to know it exists.

Monsters with Calculators

If you invest outside an RRSP or a RRIF, you'll have to share your capital gains, interest earnings, and dividends with the tax man.

Naturally, the tax is calculated differently on each kind of investment income. (If it were too simple, we wouldn't need all those office buildings full of bureaucrats.)

Your marginal tax rate plays a role too. (I've already talked about this. If you want to hear about it again, you're staying indoors too much.)

You can arrange your investments so that you pay the least amount of tax possible. This is called minimizing your tax risk. Accountants in suits make a very good living doing this all day, every day, for their clients. At night, for a change of pace, they go home and spread peanut butter all over their heads.

Monsters with Calculators in Action

If you make $40,000 a year from your job, and you earn $1,000 in interest from a Canada Savings Bond, $1,000 in capital gains from your stock mutual fund, and $1,000 in dividends from preferred stocks, all held outside your RRSP or RRIF, here's what you'll have to pay in tax:

➤ CSB interest: $1,000 x 42% = $420

➤ Mutual fund capital gain: $1,000 x 31% = $310

➤ Stock dividends: $1,000 x 25% = $250

As you can see, the best tax treatment comes from dividends, followed by capital gains and then interest income.

Fixed Income Blues Revisited

In the example above, our $1,000 in interest from a CSB turns into $580 after taxes. With inflation, that $580 will likely lose even more value. Also, your fixed-income investment is locked in for up to five years. But the tax rate keeps changing in the meantime. If you get a raise in pay, for example, you enter a higher tax bracket. The government can simply raise taxes. All this reduces your income from your fixed-rate investment even further. (Do you get the feeling that I don't like a steady diet of fixed-rate investments?)

Monster Doing the Cha-cha

Say you bought shares in a stock mutual fund for $10 a share, outside of your RRSP or RRIF, and the stock market went down and down and down (as it does sometimes). If you then sold those shares a year later for $7 each, you'd take a capital loss of $3 a share.

Capital losses can be used for tax purposes only to offset taxable capital gains. You can't use them to reduce your total taxable income.

And if you think I'm going to sit here and babble about taxes all day, forget it. If you're that bored, go read the telephone book.

Monsters with Degrees

One economist says the market's going up. Another says the market's going down. A third says the other two are all wrong and nothing much is going to happen. Which one should you listen to?

The one who confirms what you already know.

Ultimately, you have to know enough to make your own decisions. The advice of others can help, but you make the final decision. And you pay the price or reap the reward.

A Brief Definition

Economist: an expert who will know tomorrow why the things he predicted yesterday didn't happen today.

What Is Stock Market Risk?

The stock market goes up, and the stock market comes down. That's good, normal, and healthy.

Between 1946 and 1990, the market declined significantly 14 times. Those periods of decline lasted from a few months to two years, and the biggest drop occurred over a 23-month period from January 1973, to December 1974, when the Dow fell 45%.

Keep the Faith

Despite those 14 major declines, you would have made money in the market if you'd held on to your investments, even if you bought them at their peak.

The last four major peaks in the market occurred in 1969–70, 1973–74, 1981–82, and 1987. If you'd invested $5,000 at each of those market peaks, your $20,000 total investment would have grown to $150,000 by 1994. Considering that you'd invested during the worst possible times over the past quarter century, that's not bad.

So when should you start investing? Now.

Aren't You Glad You've Read This?

Over the short term, investors in the stock market will lose. That's just the way it is.

Stock market investing is not a short-term activity. If you want a short-term activity, try bungee-jumping.

Over the long term, a stock will usually perform just as an investor expects it to. But it won't perform at the expected times.

Because of this, the typical investor will purchase a stock only to see it start dropping in value within minutes. Two weeks later, as the stock continues its death-defying nose-dive into oblivion, the investor sells out of fear, having lost a good portion of the original investment. Shortly after the sale, the stock starts to rise again.

Naturally, you won't do that, because you've read this book.

The Risk Thermometer, from Hot to Cold

High Risk Investments (or Whew, I'm steamin')

Commodities

Currencies

Options

Precious metals

Common stocks

Preferred stocks

Bonds

Mutual funds

Money market funds

GICs

Bank savings accounts

Canada Savings Bonds

Treasury bills

Low Risk Investments (or Brrrrrrr, my toe just fell off)

Read It and Reap

➤ No matter where you invest your money, you'll find risk.

➤ The larger the risk, the larger your potential reward.

➤ There are many different types of risk.

➤ Purchasing power risk occurs when inflation eats away at your investment profits.

➤ The more uncertain we are about the level of interest rates in the future, the higher the risk if we lock in at today's rate.

➤ Political risk rises when governments become unstable.

➤ Social risk lead to changes in production or consumption.

➤ Currency risk affects your foreign investments, as exchange rates change.

➤ Economist risk occurs when you let someone else make your investment decisions for you.

➤ When the stock market declines, your investments lose their value. But the market will pick up again. It always has. It always will. Or my name is Elvis Presley. (Yay-yay, I'm all shook up.)

➤ Before you invest in anything, make sure you understand all the potential risks and rewards.

Chapter 13

Investment Strategies: The Game Plan

> ## In This Chapter
> ➤ Some years are better for investing than others
> ➤ What's so special about 19.4%?
> ➤ The presidential election cycle
> ➤ The best six months to invest in the stock market

Buy Low, Sell High

The surest way to make money from investing is to buy low and sell high. There you have it, folks. Let's go bowling.

Buy High, Sell Low

Unfortunately, many of us do the opposite. We buy high and sell low. Why do we act like such foolish ninnies?

Out of fear. We're afraid to get in. So we wait until the price of our selected investment has risen before we buy.

And once we're in, we're afraid to get out. So we watch the price of our investment fall before we finally sell.

This is not a good way to make money.

Some Better Ways to Make Money

Here are some investment strategies that will help you to buy low and sell high. Most of them involve equity investments and mutual funds.

Dollar Cost Averaging: The Steady Eddy Theory

This sounds complicated. Most discussions about investments do. But it's actually one of the best strategies for a beginning investor, and one of the easiest to understand.

Here's how it works: Instead of investing all your money in one shot, you invest a fixed amount at regular intervals. You decide when and how much to invest.

You can invest $100 every two weeks, for example, or $500 a month for five months, or $1,000 every three months for a year.

With each round, you buy only as many shares as your money will pay for. No more, no less. So you automatically buy more shares when their price is low and fewer shares when their price is high.

Steady Eddy in Action

For example, let's say you have $500 to invest in mutual funds. Instead of investing it all at once, you invest $100 a month for five months.

➤ In January the fund sells at $10 a share, so you pay $100 for 10 shares.

➤ In February, the fund trades at $5 a share. Your $100 investment now buys 20 shares.

➤ In March, the share price edges back to $7.50. You buy 13$\frac{1}{3}$ shares for $100.

➤ In April, the share price is back up to $10. Once again you buy 10 shares.

➤ In May, things really pick up. Your fund's share price rises to $15. With $100, you can buy only 6$\frac{2}{3}$ shares.

So where do you stand now?

You stand tall, my friend.

Come, let us go now, and calculate.

Funky Calculation

You have a total of 60 shares. (Add them up if you don't believe me.)

If you'd invested your entire $500 when your fund was selling at $10 a share, you'd have bought only 50 shares.

At $15 a share, they'd now be worth $750. (Trust me. Or figure it out yourself. In this chapter, no more math. Read my lips.)

Instead, following the Steady Eddy theory of dollar cost averaging, your 60 shares are worth a total of $900.

You're $150 ahead of the game.

Tall. Really tall.

Is This Magic, Mike?

No, this isn't magic. It results from investing a fixed amount of money at regular intervals.

As I said before, you automatically buy more shares when the price is low and fewer shares when the price is high. (Listen up, Ron. I don't want to have to say this again.)

Maximum Mike Speaks

In our example, we applied our theory over five months. But to really maximize your gains, you should invest a consistent amount, on a monthly basis, over a much longer period. The point is: be consistent.

You Have to Stick It Out!

To invest successfully using dollar cost averaging, you have to commit yourself to investing for the long term. Once you start, you can't cash in your chips after a month or two because you want the money for a trip to Acapulco or a hot date with your former music teacher.

Nor can you cash in when the market starts to fall. You have to stick with it.

In fact, the lower prices fall, the more bargains you'll pick up, and the faster your portfolio will grow.

LEARN AND EARN Most studies show that it's better to buy and hold rather than trying to time the market. Investors who held their shares in Peter Lynch's Fidelity Magellan Fund, for example, over a 10-year period in the 1980s earned an average 20% annual return. Investors who tried to time the market — who bought and sold units in the fund based on market timing instead of simply buying the units and holding them — lost on average 1% a year.

Double the Fun

Here's another catchy theory. It's called the Dow Doubler.

This theory is based on the fact that in almost every decade since 1890, the Dow has doubled between the beginning and the end of the decade.

➤ On April 19, 1897, the Dow hit a low for the decade of 38.49.

On September 5, 1899, it hit the high for the decade of 77.61, an increase of 101.6%.

➤ On January 13, 1950, the Dow hit a low for the following decade of 196.81.

On December 31, 1959, the Dow reached 679.36, an increase of 242.2%.

➤ On August 12, 1982, the Dow hit a decade low of 776.92.

On December 29, 1989, it reached 2753.20, up 254.4%.

On October 11, 1990, the Dow hit a low for the decade (so far) of 2365.10. If it at least doubles before the end of the decade, as it has in every decade but two since 1890, it will hit 4730.20 before the end of 1999. (In fact, the Dow has already exceeded this mark, and it's only 1997. It broke 7000 recently, and some market participants expect it to break 10,000 before the decade's over.)

More Nifty Stats

In seven of the nine decades since 1900, the stock market hit its lowest point within the first three years of the decade. Between 1910 and 1919, the decade's low point did not occur till 1915.

In the 1970s, the low point of the decade occurred in 1974, because of the OPEC crisis.

If our theory is correct, then the stock market reached its lowest point of the 1990s on October 11, 1990.

Take Me Higher

The stock market's high points in each decade have always occurred in the later years: in 1899, for example, 1907, 1919, 1929, 1937, 1946, 1959, 1966, 1979, and 1989.

Therefore, we should expect to see this decade's high point occur in either 1997 or 1999.

In 1997, the markets reached their highest point of the decade. Some people expect them to go much higher.

The Year of the Stock

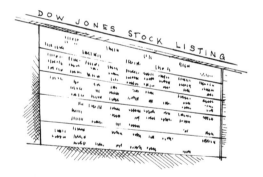

Are some years better to invest than others?

Apparently so.

I've conducted an exhaustive analysis of changes in the Dow Jones average in each year since 1891. Now I'm exhausted. Good night. Zzzzzzz.

There, now I feel better.

Some years of a decade appear to be better than others for investments.

In fact, judging by the last nine decades, the fifth year of a decade brings a consistent improvement in the Dow.

That's the fifth (5th).

In fact, a down year has never occurred in the fifth year of a decade.

This theory held in 1995. Markets began their steady rise in that year, which was a good one for investments.

In the seventh (7th) and tenth (10th) years of a decade, however, the Dow performs poorly. Once again, this trend seems to prevail in the 90s. In October 1997, the markets began to fluctuate, losing up to 10% of their value in a brief period before regaining it again.

That Ol' Magic Number: 19.4%

When the S&P 500 Index declines by 19.4%, it provides a good opportunity for investors to buy. Over the following year, there's a better-than-average chance that the market will rise significantly.

➤ On February 18, 1993, for example, the S&P 500 declined by 19.4%. A year later, the S&P 500 had risen by 87%.

➤ On May 28, 1962, the S&P 500 fell by 19.4%. A year later, it had risen again by 26%.

It doesn't always happen. On November 26, 1973, the S&P 500 fell by 19.4%. A year later, it had fallen by 28%. (People really hated this theory on that day. I wore dark glasses and a Mr. Ed suit in case I ran into someone who'd heard this theory from me.)

But out of 19 occasions since 1932 when the S&P 500 has declined by 19.4%, it has risen during the following year 14 times, and in 11 of those years, it has risen by double-digit figures.

The Presidential Shuffle

In every term of a U.S. president, there occur some good years for investors and some bad years. Taken altogether, these constitute the presidential cycle.

Each presidential cycle lasts four years.

A-one...

The first year in the cycle is the post-election year. In that year, the president bumbles along, getting used to the office, looking for the key to the presidential washroom, forgetting his phone number, stuff like that. He also has to pay for all the stupid promises that his predecessor made in the hope of getting elected. (Sometimes he's his own predecessor, and he has to pay for his own stupid promises.) People tend to forgive him. The markets perform poorly.

...And a-two...

The second year is the mid-term year. Now he knows how to find the peanut butter when he sneaks into the kitchen at night for a sandwich. But he still hasn't found the keys to the wine cellar. People aren't so forgiving, because he's still not doing much and he's been around for a year already. The markets perform poorly.

...And a-three...

The third year is called the pre-election year. Now things start to pick up. The president still doesn't know what he's doing. But he knows how to make himself look good. And he wants to get re-elected. What's the best way to get re-elected? Try to make everybody rich, and let them think you did it.

Stock markets perform almost four times better in this year of the cycle than in the previous two years.

...And a-four

The last year in the cycle is the election year. The president pulls out all the stops. You want money, he's got money. You want a highway, he'll build you a highway. You want a dog, here's my dog.

The market goes gangbusters again.

And the Numbers, Please

Over the past 27 U.S. presidential administrations, the stock market gained a total of 148% during the post-election and mid-term years.

In the pre-election and election years — the last two years — of each administration, the stock market has gained a total of 474%.

Do you still think I'm kidding?

Ok, Here's More Proof

Throughout every four-year cycle since 1916, the low point in the stock market has occurred either in the post-election or mid-term years, except during Herbert Hoover's administration. (In those four years, as a result of the depression, the low point occurred during the election year of 1932.

Hoover lost. Who'd vote for the guy who led the country into a depression? For that matter, who'd vote for a guy named after a vacuum cleaner?)

Since 1961, the low point in every bear market has occurred during the post election or mid-term years (1962, 1966, 1970, 1974, 1978, 1982, and 1990).

My Moon's in Miami. What's Your Sign?

The best six-month period to invest in the stock market: November through April.

The worst six-month period to invest in the stock market: May through October.

Here's an amazing example, based on real data. Honest, it's true.

Two investors start with $10,000.

Moe invests only from May till October, the worst months. In the other six months she keeps her money in cash.

Curly invests only from November to April, the best months, and keeps his money in cash for the rest of the year.

They both do this for 44 years, from 1949 to 1992. (These people are nothing if they're not consistent. Every day for 44 years they ate a bowl of the same kind of cereal.)

At the end of 44 years:

Moe, who invested in the bad months and whose real name is Motilda, had gained $5,083.11.

Curly, the bald guy, who invested in the good months, had gained $185,234.62.

Holy Toledo, I say.

"Yumpin' yimminy," says Moe, who's Swedish. "For long time, I've been a yerk."

January: Gonna Start the Year Off Fine...

When it comes to the stock market, January is a very special month. That's because the performance of the stock market in January indicates its performance over the following 11 months.

Between 1947 and 1996, the S&P 500 index increased in each of 29 years by more than 1% in January. In each of those years, the stock market's annual return was positive. And in 23 of those years, the return from February through December exceeded the January return.

The one exception was 1987. That year, as a result of the market crash in October, the return for the entire year was only 5.7%, compared to an increase of 13.2% in January.

Small Is Beautiful. OK, Would You Believe Good Looking? Not Ugly? Better Than a Poke in the Eye with a Burnt Stick? At Least in January

During the month of January, the stocks of small companies outperform the stocks of big companies.

In Canada and the U.S. alike, this has occurred in all but three of the last 50 years (those years were 1969, 1973, and 1990, when small-company stocks took a drubbing).

Whenever small-company stocks get hammered badly during a year, then the following January is usually a good time to invest in them. The ones that perform best are the smaller companies whose stocks are included in mutual funds such as the Altamira Select American Fund and the Everest Special Equity Fund.

Nine to Five, Monday to Friday

The best day of the week to buy stocks is Friday.

The worst day is Monday.

The best 60 minutes to buy stock is the last hour in each trading day.

Uncle Mike's Hottest Tip of the Day

The last trading day of each month and the first four trading days of each new month generate more profits than all the rest of the days in the month combined.

If, between 1987 and 1991, you'd purchased equity mutual funds on the day preceding the last trading day of each month and then sold your shares at the close of the 4th trading day of the new month, you would have beaten a buy and hold strategy. (That's nothing fancy. You buy. You hold. That's it. A no-brainer.)

A $10,000 nest egg invested in re-peated five-day patterns, beginning in 1987, would have grown to $18,292 by 1991.

Using a buy-and-hold strategy, it would have grown to only $17,217.

An Even Hotter Tip (Don't Burn Yourself on This One)

This five-day switching strategy gets even better if you invest on the two trading days before the U.S markets close for a holiday. These holidays are:

New Year's, Presidents' Day, Memorial Day, Independence Day, Labor Day, Thanksgiving, and Christmas.

How to Do It

You will be investing only five days a month, and you will be switching frequently between stock funds and money market funds. (Money market funds are basically cash funds. Come on, you remember. I told you that back in the chapter on mutual funds.)

With all this switching, you should invest only in no-load funds to avoid commission costs.

In addition, you'll be investing in stock funds only a quarter of the time. So your risk is very limited. You should seriously consider using 50% margin (that means borrow more money, equivalent to 50% of your initial investment. I explained this, too. Boy, what have you been doing? Using this book to prop up the goldfish bowl?) to in-crease your profits.

This strategy works equally well for U.S. and Canadian funds.

DOLLARS AND SENSE
$¢$¢$¢$¢

Investment managers disagree about the ideal investment strategy. (That's why there are so many of them, of course.) Some say passive manage-ment — investing in index funds, for example — com-bines the best returns with the most peace of mind for an investor. Others say that active management — pick-ing investments based on market trends, etc. — while apparently more risky, pro-duces better returns. And it's more fun, too.

Now for the Bad News

Most mutual funds will not allow you to buy and sell so frequently. Besides, over the long term, a simple strategy of dollar cost averaging (I explained that one way back at the beginning of this chapter, while you were drawing little faces in the margins) will generate better results.

Yet Another Trading Strategy

According to financial writer Christopher Byron, you can beat the markets by investing equally in units of the top 10 no-load, all-equity mutual funds every month. Over a 20-year period beginning in 1976, according to his computer calculations, a $10,000 investment moved month by month into the top 10 funds would have averaged an annual return of 18%, compared to the Dow's average return of 13%.

You Can't Beat General Motors

By looking at a single stock — General Motors — you can figure out how the entire market will move. That's because what's good for General Motors is good for the rest of the economy.

The reverse is also true: What's bad for General Motors is bad for the economy.

Although far from perfect, GM frequently leads the rest of the market at important tops and bottoms.

If GM is hitting new highs, it's unlikely that a bear market will occur. If GM is wallowing in red ink, it's not likely that you'll see a bull market.

Two Steps Forward and One Step Back

Almost every time the Dow gains at least 10% a year in two consecutive years, the stock market then takes a nose-dive.

In fact, between 1897 and 1993, the Dow Jones Industrial Average has recorded double-digit gains during two consecutive years on 18 occasions. It did it again between 1995 and 1997.

Following 18 of these 19 rises, the stock market declined.

It likely happens because the market needs to cool down. But it's worth remembering, so you can get out while the getting's good. (Did I say that? Dang me, pass the corn liquor, Chester.)

Read It and Reap

➤ At regular intervals — once a month, say — you should invest a fixed amount of money into mutual funds, no matter how your investments are performing. This strategy automatically separates your emotions from your investments.

➤ In almost every decade, the Dow has doubled from an initial low at the beginning to an ultimate high towards the end. If the decade's low occurred in 1990, then the Dow should reach at least 4730 before the end of 1999.

➤ The best years to be invested are the 5th (1995) and 8th (1998) years of a decade. The worst years are usually the 10th (2000) and the 7th (1997) years.

➤ Excellent buying opportunities usually occur after the S&P 500 Index has fallen by 19.4%.

➤ The cycle of presidential elections influences the stock market and the economy.

➤ The two best years are the pre-election (1995) and election (1996) years. Most declines tend to occur during the post-election (1993) and mid-term (1994) years.

➤ The best six months to be invested in the stock market are November through April. The worst six months are May through October.

➤ If the stock market is up in January, then there's a good chance that the rest of the year will show positive results.

➤ The best days to invest are the last trading day of each month and the first four trading days of the new month.

➤ After two consecutive years of double-digit increases in performance, the Dow usually declines.

Wills: Parting Shots

In This Chapter

What Do You Mean, I Can't Take It with Me?

As far as anyone knows, we can enjoy our money only while we're alive. And none of us knows how long that might be. You might live to be 97. Some people do. You might also die tomorrow. Some people do that, too.

No one can predict with any certainty the length of time that each of us has to grope and stumble around the planet. And as we learned early in this book, uncertainty is the bane of all investors.

A will gives us another chance to eliminate uncertainty from our financial lives. We may not know exactly when we'll bog off. But we can know exactly where our money goes when we do. And we can rest assured that the government won't take it all, as long as we have a will.

Over our lifetimes, we can all build a small fortune. At the end of the day, do you want your small fortune to go to your loved ones or the provincial government? Do you want to force your family into a courtroom to battle it out with a bunch of lawyers to see who gets what?

If you don't, it's your responsibility to make a will. The little time it takes now can save your family thousands of dollars in expensive litigation.

Looney Lingo

INTESTATE describes the financial condition of a person who dies without a will. (Irrelevant is another good word.) TESTATE is the term used to describe a person who dies with a will. (It all depends on your point of view, but irrelevant seems to apply here, too.)

Accidents Happen, But Not to Your Money

What would happen to your money if you were accidentally killed in a car crash tomorrow? Would your assets be dispersed in an orderly fashion? Would your family know exactly what assets you own? How about those shares in Acme Buggy Whips you bought last year from weird Uncle Harry? What about those gold bars you keep locked in the safety deposit box? Do you have a record of your entire estate? Do you know how much you are currently worth or how much you'll be worth later? That's where your will comes in.

What Is a Will?

A will is your plan for how you want your assets to be dispersed after your death. It's basically a list of the individuals or institutions who will get your assets when you die.

Two Main Types

There are two types of will: outright disposition and trust.

1. An outright disposition will names the beneficiaries who will receive your assets. The disposition of the assets usually occurs as soon as possible after your death.

2. A trust will places the assets inside a trust for the beneficiary. The trust contains two basic parts:

   ➤ The capital portion: the assets that are held inside the trust until the trust is dissolved.

   ➤ The income portion: the assets that will provide a regular income to the beneficiary.

When the trust is dissolved, the ultimate beneficiary receives all the assets. Trust wills are frequently left for children who, upon reaching a certain age, receive all the assets within the trust to spend as they please.

All I Own Is in My Suitcase

Let's start big and work our way down: Do you own a house? How about a car? What about life insurance? A watch? Okay, how about those boots from Mexico?

The point is, you may be worth more than you think.

It's Your Choice

You wouldn't want the government to manage your money for you now. Nor would you want the government to manage your money after you die. But it will, unless you designate a person to act as the executor and/or trustee of your estate.

Without a will, the court will designate an executor for you. And the government-appointed executor may or may not be the best person to do the job. As a result, your assets may not be distributed to your family and friends as you had planned.

What Does the Executor Do?

The executor makes sure that the provisions of your will are carried out. For example, the executor has to prove to the courts that the will is valid. This is known as probating the will. The executor is also responsible for:

➤ burying or disposing of your remains;

➤ collecting any money owed to the estate;

➤ paying all the debts owed by the estate (including income and estate taxes);

➤ providing a list of the deceased's assets; and

➤ distributing the assets to the beneficiaries in accordance with the will.

Who Should I Select as the Executor?

You can name one or more people as executors. The person (or people) you select should be honest, intelligent, and preferably younger than you.

Does the Executor Receive a Fee?

The standard fee for the administrative services of the executor is approximately 4% of the value of the estate, providing that the assets are quickly distributable. However, if the assets are held inside a trust, then the trustee receives a care-and-management fee of approximately $1/4$% each year based on the average market value of the estate. In addition, the trustee is usually allowed 5% per year of any income earned inside the trust.

These fees can sometimes be substantial. So depending on the value of your estate, it makes sense to select someone whom you'd like to receive the money.

Should I Choose My Bank as Executor of My Estate?

Most banks have trust departments that will act as executor for your estate, and many people chose to go this route. However, if your will is not complex, then you should consider a close friend or relative to act as executor.

If the executor is already familiar with your assets and beneficiaries, then so much the better. What you want to avoid is an executor with a conflict of interest.

Providing your children are over age 18, you should seriously consider giving them a role in the process. Not only will it be good experience for them in handling the assets, it will also save administrative fees.

Probate Fees

If an estate is worth more than $25,000 to $30,000, you'll usually have to probate the will before the assets can be transferred. This means a court will have to certify that the will is valid, so that the transfer agent isn't held liable for handing over the family jewels to Aunt Matilda when they really should have gone to Cousin Lou.

In particular, financial institutions will not hand over cash, stocks, bonds, or other investments, within or outside of an RRSP, unless their value is below $25,000 to $30,000, without first demanding that a will be probated. They may hand over such investments to a surviving spouse. But if you're a more distant relative, you're out of luck.

Of course, it costs money to probate a will, and every provincial government knows it. In Ontario, for example, the NDP government raised probate fees in 1992 to 1.5% of an estate's value without telling anyone. In Newfoundland, you pay $50 for the first $1,000 and $4 per additional $1,000. In Quebec, you don't have to probate the will, because the Napoleonic code requires wills to be notarized.

How to Avoid Probate

As soon as governments raise fees to probate a will, people find ways to avoid them. Here are a few suggestions:

1. Hold assets jointly. Put bank accounts, investments, etc. in the name of you and your spouse or children. For obvious reasons, you should be on good terms with them. Otherwise, your assets may end up in Hawaii, along with your spouse.

2. Put your assets in trust. Properly structured, a trust enables the

DOLLARS AND SENSE $¢$¢$¢$¢

You can leave what you want to whomever you want, only if it's not owned jointly by you and your spouse or another person. Joint ownership takes precedence over a will.

proceeds of your assets to pass to your beneficiaries tax-free and without probate fees. But you should contact an estate lawyer or trust company to make sure you structure the trust properly.

3. Give your assets away. This may sound silly, but if you give your property and investments away before you die, your survivors won't have to pay probate fees and other charges when you're gone.

Now for the Lawyers

One of the most popular choices for an executor is your lawyer. However, it is important to note that while lawyers may have superior knowledge of the administrative processes involved, they have little if any professional training when it comes to investing the funds.

On the other side of the coin, your accountant has professional training in taxes and estate planning, but lacks the administrative know-how of a lawyer.

If your will requires trusts to be set up and administered, then you should consider a trust company to act as trustee.

What Does the Trustee Do?

The trustee is responsible for administering a trust as long as it remains in force.

Trust companies are qualified to administer and invest the funds in a competent manner. On the other hand, they are notoriously conservative money managers. In addition, beneficiaries often feel uncomfortable with the impersonal service that they receive from a trust company.

What Should My Will Contain?

Here's the content of a basic will:

➤ Your name, address, and occupation;

➤ An explanation of how you want your assets to be distributed;

➤ Your signature and the date on which you signed the will;

➤ A note stating that you are revoking all of your previous wills;

➤ The name of the person (or persons) whom you would like to act as executor(s) of the estate. You should also select a contingency person, just in case the first person(s) selected can't do the job.

➤ If you have any special requests such as leaving money to your favourite charity or donating your eyes to science, then you should indicate them in your will.

➤ A contingency clause to cover the distribution of your assets in the event that the primary beneficiary dies at the same time as you do.

➤ The signatures of two witnesses (who are not beneficiaries) and their initials on each page of the will and on any changes made to the will.

Should I Ever Change My Will?

Absolutely! Over time our circumstances change. We may get married, divorced, or have children, in which case you have to assign new beneficiaries. So it's prudent to review your will on a regular basis (at least every five years).

If you plan on getting married, you should note that, in most cases, marriage automatically revokes any previous wills made by the two partners. But separation or divorce does not revoke a will unless a clause in the will specifically says that it should.

Death-tax provisions may change, which could affect the distribution of your assets.

If you decide to revise your will, you do not have to consult with any of the previously named beneficiaries.

Where Should I Keep My Will?

The best place to keep your will is with your lawyer. That way, in the event of your death, it can be easily retrieved.

You should also keep an unsigned copy of the will in your files at home.

Should a Husband and Wife Have Separate Wills?

Yes. Even if one partner does not have a career or very many assets in his or her own name, the person should still have a will.

For example, if the husband alone has a will, then his wife will receive all of his assets upon his death. However, if she then passed away before she had time to make a will, then the government decides what to do with the assets. Presumably you didn't elect a government to meddle in your personal affairs.

Do-it-yourself or Not?

If you broke your leg, would you try to set it yourself? Probably not. You'd seek out a qualified physician. The same reasoning applies to your will.

Writing your own will is usually a mistake. For one thing, beneficiaries usually end up paying a lot of money to lawyers as they try to sort out all the technicalities.

When Does a Will Become Effective?

If you have a will, it becomes effective as soon as you die. This can be a big advantage to your heirs, who otherwise wouldn't receive any assets for a long period.

If you don't have a will, all the assets will be temporarily tied up, for months or even for years. Meanwhile, bills may need to be paid and your estate managed. But there will be nobody to do it, because you didn't take the time to prepare your will.

In addition, it usually costs more to administer an estate without a will.

If You and Your Spouse Both Die, Who Looks After the Children?

Have you decided upon a guardian to look after your children in case you and your spouse both die?

Most people select the child's grandparents for the job. In fact, this isn't your best choice. That's because the grandparents are older. If they receive guardianship of your children and then pass away shortly after, the children suffer.

A better choice is to find a younger couple you trust. But make sure that they're up for the job.

What Is a Living Will?

It's not unusual for a loved one to require care to survive. But how much care is enough?

Do you want to be kept alive by artificial means? Do you want to be resuscitated after you've stopped breathing? Do you want to be kept alive even though you're in a coma and unlikely ever to regain full consciousness?

With a living will, you can relieve your family of these agonizing decisions. A living will simply describes the level of care you want if you become terminally ill. Your lawyer can help you draft it.

Power of Attorney: More Than a Loud Voice

If you couldn't manage your own finances, who could manage them for you? The person you select gets power of attorney over your finances.

If you're mentally incapable of administering your own affairs, the person to whom you've given power of attorney can take complete control of your financial affairs. He or she can sign cheques, allocate dividend payments to your bank accounts, and make other financial decisions on your behalf.

Once again, a lawyer can handle the paperwork when you designate someone to hold power of attorney.

The End of the Road

At some point you should clarify your wishes with your spouse, your children, and your executor about the disposal of your body. You may want to be buried or cremated or donate your body to science. You're in a better position to make these decisions when you're still alive and healthy than when you're not.

If you plan to bequeath your body to a university medical faculty, you should contact the university for the necessary forms. You should also obtain the forms required to donate your eyes to an eye bank and your organs to a hospital transplant program.

Facts for a Buck

If you really care about your funeral and all the other details associated with your death, put them in writing. Don't assume that your family will carry out your wishes, even if you've told them a hundred times what you want. (How many times did you tell your son to wash his hands before dinner? Did he do it?)

You should also tell your spouse, children, and executor if you want a memorial service, where you would like it to be held, and under whose auspices.

The more clearly you convey your wishes, the less confused your survivors will be when the time comes to make all these decisions.

Otherwise, they may take it for granted that you would like a priest to preside at your funeral, simply because you're Catholic. You may not agree.

Parents at the End of the Road: A Checklist

When your parent dies, you'll be amazed at all the details that you have to deal with. Some of them have to be addressed immediately: Does your parent want a funeral? Who will conduct it? What arrangements have you made to transfer the body from the place of death to the funeral home? Do you want to place an obituary notice in the local newspaper?

➤ Your parent may want to donate his body to a university. If so, he should have applied for and received a wallet-sized card with a phone number or a contact whom you can call at any time of the day or night to arrange for the transfer of the body. If the number isn't on the card, look in the phone book for the number of the university's anatomy department. Someone will come to pick up the body within hours of your call. In some cases, however, the university may not accept the body for research. The transfer service that makes this assessment on the spot can advise you on alternative arrangements. Or you can make your own, through a funeral home, funeral society, or basic funeral provider.

➤ If your parent wants to donate her eyes, she should have another card indicating the number to call for this procedure. Even blind people can donate their eyes: Corneas from blind people have been transplanted successfully into children.

Despite the good intentions indicated on an individual's driver's licence, a person can donate organs such as liver, heart, or kidneys only if he's receiving life support through a ventilator at the time of death. Otherwise, the organs stop functioning and cannot be used. This eliminates most potential donors. (In Ontario, for example, only two percent of all deaths qualify as potential sources of organ donations, and there are only 150 donations a year.)

➤ Finally, if your parent has selected you as executor, you have to close bank accounts, terminate pension plans, apply for death benefits, notify the provincial registrar and health authorities, and submit final income tax returns. (If you feel like screaming when your parent dies, wait till you fill out his last income tax form.) To do all this, you'll need a death certificate, which you get from the undertaker or funeral home (not the attending physician). You'll also need your parent's social security number. (If you can't find the card, the number is indicated on your parent's tax returns.)

➤ The undertaker will also provide you with the necessary forms to apply for death benefits. However, to terminate Old Age Pension and Canada Pension Plan benefits, you have to phone the nearest office of the Income Security Programs branch of Human Resources Development Canada. The number's listed in the blue pages of your phone book. You also have to contact the administrators of any private pension plans to which your parent has contributed. They will send you a final accounting and, at the appropriate time, they'll send you receipts for income tax purposes.

➤ Paying income tax is probably the last act you'll perform on behalf of your parent. You have to contact Revenue Canada and ask for a "tax return for deceased persons." A nice man or woman will record the details and send you a form. You have until the following year to submit the return on behalf of your parent.

Read It and Reap

➤ Everybody 18 years of age and older should have a will.

➤ If you don't have a will then the government will decide what happens to your assets.

➤ Always hire a competent lawyer to prepare your will for you.

➤ Make sure that your family knows where all your important documents are located.

➤ Think carefully before deciding upon an executor of your estate. It is not a decision to be taken lightly.

➤ Make sure you review your will at least every five years.

➤ Everyone should consider granting power of attorney to a spouse or friend in the event that you become incapacitated and can't manage your finances.

➤ Don't put it off. Make an appointment with your financial planner and lawyer today.

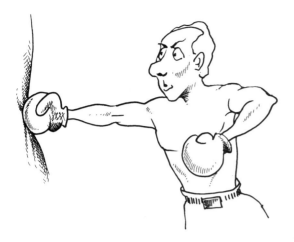

Chapter 15

Financial Planners: Keeping You in Fighting Trim

In This Chapter

➤ Financial planners

➤ Stockbrokers

➤ Why do you need one?

➤ How do you find one?

➤ What questions should you ask your financial planner?

➤ Computerized planners

This book will provide you with the basics you need to start investing. But to stay on top of things, you should seriously consider finding yourself a good coach.

These days, events that affect the financial world occur from hour to hour. And keeping on top of all the information coming down the info highway has become a full-time job.

Fortunately, it doesn't have to be your job. There are people who will do it for you, called financial planners.

A financial planner will keep you informed about your investment alternatives. A planner can answer questions like:

➤ Is the market cheap or expensive?

➤ Which mutual funds should I buy?

➤ Where can I get the highest rates of return?

➤ How can I save on my taxes?

➤ What is my investment comfort level?

A Coach by Any Other Name

Financial coaches come in all shapes and sizes. They include stockbrokers, bankers, financial planners, insurance agents, and in some instances, your lawyer and accountant. Each is an expert in his or her particular field.

Beginning investors are best advised to find a good financial planner or stockbroker.

Your Financial Travel Agent

When we take a holiday overseas, we don't always call an airline directly to book a flight. Instead, we use the services of a travel agent. A good travel agent can scan all the airlines, tell us who's flying where, when they go, and at what price.

The agent will book our flight, reserve a hotel room, and take care of the travel insurance.

Agents do all the work. All we have to do is show up at the airport.

Financial planners work in a similar fashion, helping us plan a comfortable and rewarding trip through the financial world.

Naturally it helps to know where we're going. Some of us may want tips on tax-saving strategies. Others may want life insurance advice or guidance in selecting mutual funds. We may be aiming to finance a university education or planning our retirement or our estate. In all these cases, a good financial planner can help.

Surprise of the Month: Stockbrokers Sell Stocks

Full-service stockbrokers can provide many different financial products and services. But they tend to specialize in stocks, bonds, and mutual funds.

Their firms do the research and provide you with a company's earnings, dividends, and current buy, sell, or hold recommendation.

Their advice is free, but they take a commission for every trade they make on your behalf. That fee pays for the broker's time and expertise, in addition to research reports and overhead.

It is important to remember that the stockbroker only makes money when you buy or sell investments.

Two for a Buck; For You, Fifty Cents

Discount brokers also sell stocks, bonds, mutual funds, futures, and options. They may provide investment advice, but usually it's basic stuff like "Now is a good time to plan for your retirement." Some discount brokers provide research, for a fee, but you have to draw your own conclusions. If you find that the price of kidney-bean futures has risen by three cents, while a strike has resulted in shortages of Beano, you might consider an investment in the company that makes the stuff. But you won't get any advice from the discount broker. You're on your own, bud.

> **LEARN AND EARN**
>
> You can conduct transactions with a discount brokerage like CIBC's Investor's Edge, E*Trade, Priority, or TD Green Line by telephone or by e-mail, over the Internet.

Because they provide only the bare bones of a brokerage service, discount brokers charge less for their services. But shop around. Some charge more than others.

Discount or Full-Service?

If you enjoy doing your own research and making your own investment decisions, and if you want to blame nobody but yourself for your mistakes, then you should place your trades through a discount broker.

If you're just beginning, don't have time to spend reading annual reports and financial statements, if you're just looking for some new ideas or a second opinion, or if you really want someone else to blame when the value of your shares falls into the toilet, then a full-service broker is for you.

Many investors use both. They use the full-service broker for investment advice and research reports. And if they decide to follow the broker's advice, they place the order through the broker. But if they make an investment decision on their own, they place the order through their discount broker.

Stockbrokers are regulated by provincial securities commissions and the Investment Dealers Association. The primary advantage of using a full-service broker is the extensive research about investment decisions she can provide.

Battle of the Number Crunchers: Financial Planners vs. Stockbrokers

At one time, stockbrokers sold only stocks, bonds, and mutual funds. Financial planners specialized in tax-saving strategies and advice on investment returns.

Like everything else in the financial world, that's changed. Today, many tax-wise stockbrokers can provide financial planning services to their clients as well as trading shares on their behalf. Stockbrokers now sell term deposits, GICs, mortgage-backed securities, and Treasury bills.

On the other hand, financial planners now sell mutual funds and life insurance, and some will even negotiate a home mortgage for you.

Unfortunately, the profession is unregulated, and anyone can call himself a financial planner, even if he can't calculate his own age.

To avoid mistakes — and bad planning — look for a Certified Financial Planner. These people put the initials C.F.P. after their names. Anyone with a C.F.P. designation has studied extensively and passed certified exams, cramming his head full of arcane knowledge about things that no one else in his right mind would bother to learn.

The Canadian Association of Financial Planners can help you to find a reputable financial planner.

Independent Financial Planners

An independent financial planner can provide you with the best products offered by many different companies.

Financial planners who work for a single company generally limit themselves to selling their own company's products.

And Now for the Good News: You Owe Me a Billion Dollars

Financial planners bill their clients in one of two general ways:

1. Fee only. The planner charges a one-time flat fee of 0.5% to 1% of your portfolio. But you usually need at least $50,000 to invest.

   The planner may also charge an hourly fee.

2. Commission only. The financial planner gets paid only when she sells one of her financial products. The financial planner is compensated either by a commission paid directly by you (usually 3% to 5% of the amount invested) or by a mutual fund company in the form of a finder's fee.

   This is by far the most popular method of paying a financial planner.

Look for Results

A financial planner may charge you nothing at all and be worth no more. If the planner doesn't get results, then his advice isn't worth much.

But a planner who helps you earn a profit on your money, year after year, earns his fees.

Facts for a Buck

Members of the Canadian Association of Financial Planners need two years of working experience and must have liability insurance to qualify for a CAFP designation. CAFP (www.cafp.org) provides a free consumer's guide to financial planning, including a detailed list of member planners. (To reach CAFP's Toronto head office, call 416-593-6592.)

The Hunt Begins: Finding a Financial Consultant

A friend or relative can usually refer you to a good financial consultant. If that's not possible, then call at least three financial planning or brokerage firms directly.

Always ask for the manager, and make an appointment to see him or her. Before you go, identify your investment objectives. Are you looking for growth, income, or a combination? Do you want to take risks or play it safe?

With this information, the firm's manager can place you with a financial consultant who can best meet your needs.

Whatever you do, never bring your chequebook to the initial interview. Compare at least three different firms before you lay down your money.

Questions, Questions, Questions

The planner or broker will ask you a lot of questions during your interview to find out how you want to invest your money.

But you're the one who pays the shots, so you should ask a few questions too.

1. *What are your qualifications and experience?*

   Your financial consultant should have at least three years' experience.

2. *Where do you get your financial information?*

   If the consultant says, "The daily newspaper," you've come to the wrong place. Most financial consultants receive in-house research material in addition to independent financial publications. Industry contacts, friends, and business associates may also provide them with valuable information.

   Ideally, he or she should have access to information that you don't already have.

3. *Are you a financial specialist or generalist?*

   Some financial planners may know a lot about tax-saving strategies, but nothing about the stock market. And some stockbrokers may know a lot about the stock market and nothing at all about taxes or life insurance. Look for an investment adviser who specializes in your area of interest.

4. *Do you specialize in aggressive or conservative investments?*

If you want to buy shares in Royal Bank, but the broker wants to sell you shares in Moose Pasture Mines, then you've got a problem.

Likewise, if you're young, aggressive, and ready to take the financial bull by the horns of risk (Did I really say that? Whew), you won't want a broker whose most aggressive recommendation is Bell Canada.

The financial consultant's investment style should match your investment needs.

5. *Do you have enough time to handle my account?*

If you have limited funds with which to invest (under $5,000, for example), you may have to wait in line to get advice and information from some brokers. In general, the more you have to invest, the better the service you'll receive. (This makes sense. Brokers are as greedy as the rest of us. They're not in business to save your soul.)

Some brokers don't even handle small accounts, but many others do, on the assumption that today's small account is tomorrow's big one.

Some brokers may have too many clients (about 100 is a good cut-off point).

Your broker should have time to meet with you every few months to review your portfolio.

6. *How are you compensated?*

Does the broker charge a fee for service, a commission or a finder's fee? Whatever the arrangement, make sure that the rates are competitive with those of other firms providing the same services and products.

7. *What was the best and worst advice that you ever gave?*

Listen carefully to the answer.

8. *Can you provide me with some references?*

Beware of any financial planner or broker who will not provide you with references who will attest to his or her performance.

Deposit Brokers: When Adventure Is a Four-letter Word

If you've read this far, and you'd still prefer a safe, predictable haven for your money to a more risky one, perhaps you could use the services of a deposit broker. These guys (and non-guys) look for guaranteed, safe, secure savings products for their customers, even when markets are raging and investors are becoming billionaires overnight. They'll poke around to find the best rates on a GIC, for example, or the best returns on a savings account. Most of their clients are wealthy and venerable (and probably have no interest in this book. Oh, well).

If you're venerable and rich and want to find a deposit broker, you can contact Brad Minton, the president of the 110-member Federation of Independent Deposit Brokers at 250-339-2719.

The King and His Court: How Many Advisers Do You Need?

Once your portfolio begins to grow, you may want advice from more than one source. After all, the more knowledge and information you have, the better your decisions.

All of your advisers should know the details of your entire portfolio. Otherwise, they may advise you to invest in an area where you've already stashed enough of your wad.

You Take the Wheel While I Tie My Shoelaces

Before advisers or brokers can make a trade or purchase on your behalf and with your money, they must always consult you, unless you authorize them to act on your behalf.

Never give them this authorization.

In case that wasn't clear enough, I'll say it again. Never give them this authorization.

Not Just Butter: Churning

When brokers advise you to buy and sell much more often than you should, they're trying to earn higher commissions. This is called churning. There are stronger words to describe the broker, but we won't use them here.

Report the broker immediately to the manager if you suspect this is happening.

I Want to Make a Complaint

To lodge a complaint about the quality of service that you've received from your stockbroker or financial planner, first discuss your concerns directly with the adviser. If he or she can't help, or tells you that you're a meddling scumbucket, then take your complaint to the manager or the president of the adviser's company.

Expand Your Mind: You Can Never Know Enough

Even if you have a good financial adviser, you should also do your own research. The first and easiest place to start is with your daily newspaper. The business sections of all major newspapers contain stock and mutual fund listings and timely investment articles.

The two best Canadian newspapers for business news are *The Financial Post* and *The Globe & Mail*.

LEARN AND EARN

You can find business news and information in a number of locations that you can reach through the Internet. For example, you can try:

www.imoney.com for mutual fund performance, stock quotes, and graphs.

www.investor-corner.com provides financial data accumulated over the last 10 years on 1,000 Canadian companies.

Most publicly listed companies operate their own web sites, providing financial data and performance results. Try reaching them through www.yahoo.ca.

The three best U.S. newspapers are *The Wall Street Journal*, *Investor's Business Daily*, and *Barron's*.

Adviser in a Box

You probably own a computer, and you probably know how to use it. With the right investment software and a little practice, you can learn how to track your investments, execute trades, and screen potential investment candidates with the best of them.

Tracking involves keeping tabs on your investments by purchase price, number of shares, initial and current dollar value, and other categories.

Trading, as it sounds, involves contacting a discount brokerage via modem and instructing it, electronicically, to execute a trade on your behalf.

Screening involves gathering data on a particular stock and analyzing it to see if it makes sense to buy shares in the stock.

There are more than 500 software packages currently on the market to help you perform one or all of these functions. Some of them cost as little as $20. By subscribing to an on-line database like CompuServe or America Online, you can gather historical and current stock quotes.

These packages may not make you a millionaire overnight, any more than a word processing package will turn you into a writer. But they'll make it a lot easier to figure out how your investments are performing and which stocks you'd like to choose next.

Read It and Reap

➤ When it comes to our finances, we all need a good coach.

➤ Before you talk to a financial adviser, identify your investment objectives.

➤ Interview at least three financial planning or brokerage firms before you choose a financial adviser.

➤ Don't let the suit intimidate you. You're doing the hiring, not the broker.

➤ Ask questions. Make sure your financial adviser understands your goals and objectives and has your best interests at heart.

➤ Never give your financial adviser complete discretion over your account.

➤ Educate yourself, then use your broker or financial planner for additional insight.

Index

More Great Canadian Complete Idiot's Guides!

If you liked this *Complete Idiot's Guide*, check out these other titles!

The Complete Idiot's Guide to Making Money in the Canadian Stock Market
by Christy Heady and Stephen Nelson

The Complete Idiot's Guide to Making Money in the Canadian Stock Market helps you make sense of the complicated world of finance. You will learn the best financial strategies, feel confident about investing your money, and build your wealth with the help of this exciting new guide.

346 pages
$24.95
ISBN 0-13-779134-8

The Complete Idiot's Guide to Getting Rich in Canada
by Larry Waschka and Bruce McDougall

Many Canadians want a worry-free retirement, neat stuff and the freedom of choice and security — in other words, they want to be rich! In this comprehensive new book you will learn all the essential techniques, attitudes, and perspective required to live the good life. This guide provides clear advice on how to build your personal fortune and achieve your dreams of grandeur, with ease!

352 pages
$21.95
ISBN 0-13-080127-5

The Complete Idiot's Guide to Canadian History
by Ann Douglas

You may read the newspaper every day and keep up with with all the latest information, but how much do you know about what went on way back when? When you try to remember even the basics of Canadian history does your mind go blank? Perfect for those new to this country as well as Canadians who need a refresher course, *The Complete Idiot's Guide to Canadian History* presents everything you need to know and makes learning fun, fascinating and memorable. Relive the fur trade, the War of 1812, and other historical events.

_____

270 pages
$19.95
ISBN 0-13-779126-7

The Complete Idiot's Guide to Exploring Canada
by Joe Chidley

Canada is every traveller's dream — a big, beautiful country with plenty to see and do. Boasting mountain ranges, two scenic coasts and many metropolitan centres, it has something for everyone looking for adventure and enjoyment. But Canada's vastness makes it hard to figure out where to begin your journey. *The Complete Idiot's Guide to Exploring Canada* is an easy to use, up-to-date travel guide that makes planning your trip a sure success.

_____

272 pages
$21.95
ISBN 0-13-080125-9